# DEEP FREEZE

# DEEP FREEZE
*Iceland's Economic Collapse*


**Philipp Bagus**
Rey Juan Carlos University

**David Howden**
St. Louis University — Madrid Campus

Copyright © 2011 by the Ludwig von Mises Institute

Published under the Creative Commons Attribution License 3.0.
http://creativecommons.org/licenses/by/3.0/

Ludwig von Mises Institute
518 West Magnolia Avenue
Auburn, Alabama   36832

Ph:  (334) 844-2500
Fax: (334) 844-2583

mises.org

10 9 8 7 6 5 4 3 2 1

ISBN: 978-1-933550-34-3

# Foreword

by Toby Baxendale

The two young Professors Bagus and Howden document the sad story of the Icelandic government's policy mistakes—the artificial creation of a boom, and the savage bust that was the inevitable outcome of this boom.

Little have we learned since the wisdom of Mises and Hayek showed us the way concerning business cycle theory. The former are intellectual heirs of the latter two giants of 20$^{th}$ century economics and they present the case of the small nation of Iceland, within the context of the global economy, analyzed via the lens of what has become know as the Austrian Theory of the Business Cycle, extremely well here.

This is a short book and I hope it will encourage others to write about other bigger nations: after all, we are all very much interdependent. I hope they will write via the insights of the great teachers of the Austrian School. For the majority of economists who assume that the marginal revolution has all been absorbed into mainstream economics and that the Austrian School has nothing to add on the matter, I would urge them to pause and reflect on the Austrian theory of the business cycle—the case-proven status of it as outlined in this book—with reference to Iceland and think about what they are doing when they advise governments to artificially "stimulate demand."

I write this as someone very much involved in the Icelandic economy. As a wholesaler and retailer of fresh fish in the UK, Iceland is probably ten percent of my lines of supply. For some twenty years, I have dealt with the various parts of the Icelandic fishing community and their buccaneering fishermen turned bankers. Be under no illusions, these are hardy people. Much as I do not intend to make a generalization about a population, these are the heirs of the Vikings: they live in an extremely harsh environment and they will bounce back very quickly if allowed to by their government.

One successful cod and prawn processor was telling me that, although he was bust, as most Icelandic companies are, he remembers that it was only thirty-four years ago that he used to stay with his grandfather in a stone-and-grass-built house, with no heating and fresh running water. This current economic collapse would be a setback in the scheme of things but that was all, according to him.

Bagus and Howden describe how the Icelandic business community were encouraged to borrow in Japanese Yen and Swiss Francs with their attractive low interest rates. Commeth the bust, I was asked to "rescue" many of these firms. The key problem with the banks essentially owning all the bankrupt highly leveraged businesses (that were and are essentially good ocean harvesting fishing businesses, albeit loaded over the eyeballs in debt), was that they were in turn owned by the government. The government, not wanting the lifetime of fish quotas to get into the hands of a nasty foreign creditor, would not and still does not allow them to go bust. This irresponsible action on behalf of the government will ensure these zombified fish companies will continue undead for many years to come. The reality is that they need new fresh capital and the only way they can get this is for the government to let undead businesses go bust and to allow a reorganization in their management and capital structure to take place. No one in a zillion years will buy companies with more than 30 times leverage to pre-tax earnings!

Seeing the demise of formerly solvent companies suddenly becoming insolvent with borrowing in Swiss Francs and Yen was something I would not wish upon anyone. Whilst individuals have personal responsibility for their actions, if the Icelandic State is setting the conditions so that the rational course of action is to participate in the boom, then culpability must fall, in the final analysis, with the originators of the problem: the Icelandic Central Bank.

The fact is that the whole economy of Iceland collapsed and the Central Bank of Iceland, who set the scene to cause the collapse, still exists in its current form. Will they ever learn? If they were a private company, they would have wound up with their assets sold to the highest bidder. "Be done with them all," should be the cry, these failed, manipulating regulators. This is, clearly, what we should be saying to all Central Banks around the world.

While the central bank was fiddling as their collapsed economy, I remember fishermen coming into port after trips at sea with a hold full of valuable fish deteriorating minute by minute. Buyers like my company could not transact with them, as we could not convert sterling or euro into krónur (the market did not exist). At one point in time, my Finance Director and I had a case packed with sterling, dollars and euro ready to get on a plane and physically give cash in exchange for fish. Fortunately, we found a very accommodating travel agent, who could not believe his luck, that there were these two English guys with hard currency who actually wanted some of his "worthless" Icelandic krónur. For him, Santa Claus had arrived early. We did a deal with him and used the stock of money (krónur) with which he had been lumbered to facilitate the purchase of fresh fish; needs must be met in these circumstances. In fairness to the Icelandic Central bank, they told us (20 minutes before officially going bust via email) not to wire them money to supply to our fishermen as they themselves were going bust!

To make matters worse the new Icelandic government has decided in its infinite wisdom that the people of Iceland own the fish quotas. Over 20 years, 5 percent of these quotas will be confiscated off the current quota owners each year so they can never be owned by foreigners! What the Iceland government does not realize is that a banker in Geneva or Tokyo does not want fish quota, he wants cash! In reality these foreign bankers will sell this quota back to the Icelandic fleet owners, who will be willing buyers at a discount. I hope that reason will prevail and these fishing quotas be privatized rather than the current long-term trajectory with the Icelandic fishing industry being zombified.

Chaos is never a good economic policy. Central planners, as with central banks, can no more set the cod price of the day than they can set the price of money. Do not interfere with the peoples' money. In the case of Iceland, if left alone they would have been chugging along with a great source of sustainable raw material—the fish. This is fished in the some of the world's finest fishing grounds. They also possess a tremendous source of cheap geothermal power, which can be slowly and painstakingly used to rebuild a wonderfully long-term, enduringly prosperous economy.

Enjoy the read.

# Contents

1 Introduction 1

2 Maturity Mismatching 7

3 The IMF, Moral Hazard, and the Temptation of Foreign Funds 27

4 Currency Mismatching 37

5 The Consequences of the Boom: Malinvestments 51

6 A Timeline of the Collapse 73

7 Why the Fed Could Save Its Bankers, But the CBI Could Not 95

8 The Necessary Restructuring 105

9 Concluding Remarks 115

# Graphs

1. Central Bank of Iceland policy rate (percent)    14
2. Icelandic money supply (January 2000–October 2010, million krónur)    19
3. Funding gap: big three banks (as at June 2008, in million krónur)    23
4. Interest rate gap of the CBI to the BoJ, ECB and the Fed (in percent)    39
5. Euro area, Japanese yen, and U.S. dollar M2 (January 2001 = 100)    43
6. Net domestic and foreign assets of the banking system (million króna)    44
7. Foreign funding gap: big three banks (million krónur)    48
8. Housing prices (2000 = 100)    60
9. Average yearly house price appreciation (percent)    61
10. Balance of Trade (million krónur)    66
11. Value of securities outstanding (2000 = 100)    67
12. New automobile registrations    68

## Graphs

13. Icelandic Stock Market (OMX All Share Index, January 1, 2000–December 1, 2010, krónur) — 72
14. Króna exchange rates — 76
15. OMX Iceland All-Share Index (daily close, September 22–October 22, 2008, krónur) — 88
16. Housing prices (July 2008 to October 2010, capital area single flat houses = 100) — 90
17. Central Bank of Iceland liquidity ratio (August 2007–September 2009) — 101
18. Funding gaps, Central Bank of Iceland and big three banks combined (million krónur). — 102
19. Average annual hours worked per employee (2000 = 100) — 110
20. Public Opinion on Icelandic accession to the EU (August 2005–February 2010) — 120

# Tables

1. Corporate debt (percentage of GDP) — 5
2. Icelandic money supply growth (percent) — 20
3. CBI policy rate, inflation and real interest rates (2000–2008) — 45
4. Domestic and Foreign Funding Gaps (million króna, year-on-year percentage) — 46
5. The big three banks' funding gaps (million ISK) — 82

# Chapter 1

# Introduction

Following the bankruptcy of the American investment bank, Lehman Brothers, in late 2008, credit markets all over the world seized up, in a striking manifestation of the interconnectivity of the global economy. When the dust had settled, the crisis had wiped out trillions of dollars of investments, and the previously well-functioning credit markets had stalled. The most spectacular bankruptcy of the 2008 financial crisis was the collapse of Iceland's financial system. This collapse is especially intriguing as Iceland is not an underdeveloped country (it ranked third in the United Nations' 2009 Human Development Index).

During the several years leading up to the collapse, Iceland experienced an economic boom. The Icelandic financial system expanded considerably; a nation with a population only slightly larger than Pittsburgh, Pennsylvania and a physical size smaller than the American state of Kentucky erected a banking system whose total assets were ten times the size of the country's GDP. The prices of housing and stocks soared, and consequently so did Iceland's wealth. The traditional fishing-based economy was altered dramatically. Financial engineering became the preferred career path of ambitious youth, instead of the traditional natural resource management. Young men on the streets of Reykjavík were as likely to know the Black-Scholes formula as the yields from the day's salmon catch. People from all walks of life wanted to work in the banking industry. A general practitioner cited his experience in "communicating" with people daily as his key asset.[1] Young children, when asked what they wanted to grow up to be, innocently and unhesitatingly answered, "Bankers."

The banking sector became so large that it was having trouble finding enough talented and, more importantly, experienced workers in such a tiny country. The best employees of more traditional Icelandic businesses were headhunted away to work in the growing financial sector.

Then, in autumn 2008, the dream of unlimited wealth ended suddenly with the bankruptcy of the Icelandic state. The exchange rate of the Icelandic króna collapsed, the three big Icelandic banks, Landsbanki, Kaupthing and Glitnir, were nationalized, the unemployment rate soared, and the rate of price inflation reached 18 percent by the end of 2008. In a few short months, Icelanders lost not only the wealth they had accumulated during the short-lived boom, but also a good portion of the savings they had worked diligently for many years to amass. The stock market fell by 90 percent. *Statistics Iceland* reports that Reykjavík housing prices fell by over 9 percent during 2009.[2] What savings remained had changed in location and in kind. Instead of depositing their money in banks, Icelanders preferred to hold foreign currency; they rid themselves of krónur at any chance they got. They started to hoard groceries and supplies.

With their government bankrupt, Icelanders might well have experienced physical hunger had it not been for foreign help. Foreign loans to secure essential food imports came primarily from

---

[1] Armann Thorvaldsson, *Frozen Assets: How I Lived Iceland's Boom and Bust* (Chichester, UK: John Wiley and Sons, 2009), p. 147.
[2] *Statistics Iceland*

sympathetic Scandinavian countries with close historical ties to Iceland. The government instituted exchange rate regulations and controls to limit the use of foreign exchange to the purchase of newly precious imports such as food, drugs, and oil.

What made such a boom and bust possible? Common superficial analyses of Iceland's economic crisis have mirrored the analyses offered for the worldwide crisis. Analysts and journalists alike have blamed the worldwide crisis on the usual suspects: greedy bankers, inexperienced upstarts, a corrupt political elite, the deregulation of the financial system, or, more generally, the evils of capitalism. Likewise, some commentators and economists[3] have blamed Iceland's crisis on financial deregulation during the preceding decade. Gumbel contends that the free-market program of Davíð Oddsson, Prime Minister from 1991 to 2004 and a self-proclaimed fan of Milton Friedman, caused the debacle.

The problem with this explanation is that Iceland could not, by any stretch of language, be called a free market.[4] In 2007, before the crisis erupted, Icelandic taxes and contributions to social security were the ninth highest among nations in the OECD (41.1 percent of GDP).

Iceland's particular crisis, and the world's in general, was caused by the manipulations of central banks and intergovernmental organizations. Thus, in the final analysis, it was the actions of governments that brought about Iceland's financial collapse. While some point to the supposed independence of central banks from their nations' governments, few could argue that the Central Bank of Iceland, with two of its three governors direct political appointees, could be anything other than a cog in the political machine.[5] In short, the causes of Iceland's financial

---

[3]Peter Gumbel, "Iceland: The Country That Became a Hedge Fund," *CNN Money* (December 4, 2008), and Paul Krugman, "The Icelandic Post-Crisis Miracle," *The New York Times* (June 30, 2010).

[4]Philipp Bagus and David Howden, "Iceland's Banking Crisis: The Meltdown of an Interventionist Financial System," *Ludwig von Mises Institute, Daily Article* (June 9, 2009).

[5]Roger Boyes, *Meltdown Iceland: Lessons on the World Financial Crisis*

collapse are the same causes that explain the worldwide financial crisis of 2008. The main difference in Iceland's case is their magnitude. In Iceland, the economic distortions were extreme, making the country's financial structure particularly prone to collapse. Moreover, the Icelandic case contains a special ingredient that made an exceedingly rare event for a developed nation, sovereign bankruptcy, possible in the first place.

During the boom, Iceland's fiscal framework was ineffective at curtailing government expenditures.[6] Local and national governments routinely surpassed their budgets. Budget overruns became the norm in Iceland's parliament, the *Althing*, with few severe repercussions. This fiscal imbalance became a mainstay of the Icelandic public sector.

In the ten years leading up to Iceland's financial collapse, there were fantastic liberalizations in the world economy as globalization swept the planet. Benefits of these changes were widespread, with few people unaffected. However, the liberalizations were accompanied by several salient interventions that compounded their effects.

Immediately following Iceland's financial collapse in late 2008, the International Monetary Fund's Icelandic mission chief, Poul Thomsen, was asked, "What went wrong in Iceland?" He reckoned that the root cause was that a very oversized banking system was allowed to develop.[7] Thomsen went on to note that, after the Icelandic government completed the privatization of the banking sector in 2003, banks increased their assets from 100 percent of Icelandic GDP to over 1,000 percent. Though he blamed the current situation on this perceived unsustainable situation, Thomsen did not raise the question of *why* the banks could expand so rapidly.

---

*from a Small Bankrupt Island* (New York, Berlin, London: Bloomsbury USA, 2009), p. 114.

[6]Robert Tchaidze, Anthony Annett, and Li Lian Ong, "Iceland: Selected Issues," IMF Country Report no. 07/296 (2007), p. 15.

[7]Camilla Andersen, "Iceland Gets Help to Recover from Historic Crisis," *IMF Survey Magazine* 37, no. 12 (December 2, 2008).

| | |
|---|---|
| Iceland | 308 |
| Euro area[8] | 77 |
| UK[9] | 278 |
| USA | 73 |

Source: Caruanna and Chopra (2008)

Table 1: Corporate debt (percentage of GDP)

The real reasons for Iceland's collapse lie in state institutions and in intrusions by the state into the workings of the economy, coupled with the interventionist institutions of the national and international monetary systems. Iceland's crisis is the result of two banking practices that, in combination, proved to be explosive: excessive maturity mismatching and currency mismatching. While these two activities, especially maturity mismatching, are ubiquitous in modern finance, they were carried to more extreme lengths in Iceland than in other countries, making the Icelandic financial system especially fragile. Corporate debt levels exceeded 300 percent of GDP in Iceland in 2007, more than four times the level in the United States (see Table 1). The Icelandic banking sector financed roughly two-thirds of this debt, and seventy percent of it was denominated in foreign currency. Over sixty percent of Iceland's external indebtedness was of short-term durations, and ninety-eight percent of this was on account of the banking sector. While this foreign-denominated debt was mostly used to finance foreign investments, Icelandic companies with no foreign operations owed a large and growing share of this debt.[10]

The system was further weakened by the existence of an institution that serves to bail out sovereign nations on an international level: the International Monetary Fund (IMF). The implicit assurance of support by the Fund reduced the risk

---

[8]Data is for 2005.   [9]Financial liabilities.
[10]Jaime Caruanna and Ajai Chopra, "Iceland: Financial System Stability Assessment-Update," IMF country Report no. 03/368 (2008), pp. 9–10.

premium and volatility of exchange rates, and this, in turn, induced people around the world to increase funding in foreign currency. The króna enjoyed the dubious benefit of being one of the more stabilized currencies that investors turned to. Consequently, the Icelandic banks shifted from denominating their debts in krónur to undertaking foreign liabilities sponsored by the international credit expansion. The consequences of this dual arbitrage of maturities and foreign currency risk would prove to be lethal. Malinvestment and an accompanying shift of resources into the financial sector set the stage for a collapse. An increased amount of foreign-denominated financing bred malinvestments that the monetary authority could not unwind. The international liquidity squeeze of the fall of 2008 burst the financial bubble. The Central Bank of Iceland and the government tried to act as lenders of last resort, and they failed. The economy collapsed.

Despite the hardships of the past two years, there are green shoots that could grow and flourish. Recovery is not impossible, though it will require hardship and perseverance. At the end of this book, we outline a route to recovery.

Chapter 2

# Maturity Mismatching

Iceland has something in common with other developed economies that the recent economic crisis has affected: its banking system was heavily engaged in maturity mismatching. In other words, Icelandic banks issued short-term liabilities in order to invest in long-term assets. Thus, they had to continuously roll over (renew) their short-term liabilities until their long-term assets matured. If an event arose whereby Icelandic banks failed to find new borrowers to continue rolling their liabilities over, they would face a liquidity crisis and the Icelandic financial system would collapse.

Considering recent events that have exposed the riskiness of this strategy, the question that immediately comes to mind is, why did Icelandic banks engage so heavily in this risky practice in the first place? One reason is that maturity mismatching can turn out to be a very profitable business involving a basic interest arbitrage. Normally, long-term interest rates are higher than the corresponding short-term rates. A bank that sells short-term rates (borrows money short-term), while buying long-term rates (investing money long-term) may profit from the difference (the "spread") between short- and long-term rates. Yet while maturity mismatching can turn out to be profitable, it is also very risky, because the short-term debts require continual reinvestment (that is, there must be a continual "rollover"). The most extreme case of maturity mismatching is the expansion of credit by banks, when deposits (i.e., debts of zero maturity) are used to grant credit (i.e., assets of longer maturities).

For much of its history, banking abided by a "golden rule" that is still alluded to today but rarely followed: the duration to maturity of a bank's assets should correspond to that of its liabilities. Any incongruence opens the bank to risk in the event of liquidity shocks. The golden rule can be traced back at least to Otto Hübner,[1] who wrote, "If a bank is to avoid the risk of being unable to fulfill its obligations, the credit it grants must correspond with the credit it receives, not only quantitatively but also qualitatively."[2]

The golden rule was still upheld at the turn of the last century. Ludwig von Mises, building upon his German predecessor Karl Knies,[3] expanded on this sound banking rule:

> For the activity of the banks as negotiators of credit the golden rule holds, that an organic connection must be created between the credit transactions and the debit transactions. The credit that the bank grants must correspond quantitatively and qualitatively to the credit that it takes up. More exactly expressed, "The date on which the bank's obligations fall due must not precede the date on which its corresponding claims can be realized." Only thus can the danger of insolvency be avoided.[4]

---

[1] Otto Hübner, *Die Banken* (Leipzig: Verlag von Heinrich Hübner, 1854), p. 28.

[2] As translated from the original German: "Der Credit, welchen eine Bank geben kann, ohne Gefahr zu laufen, ihre Verbindlichkeiten nicht erfüllen zu können, muß nicht nur im Betrage, sondern auch in der Qualität dem Credit entsprechen, den sie genießt."

[3] Karl Knies, *Geld und Kredit*, Vol. 2 (Berlin: Weidmann'sche Buchhandlung, 1876).

[4] Ludwig von Mises, *The Theory of Money and Credit* (New Haven, Conn.: Yale University Press, [1912] 1953), p. 263. In a similar way, Murray N.

When a bank or other financial entity takes on short-term liabilities and invests them for a longer term, it violates the "golden rule."[5] While Mises does not follow up to investigate how violating this rule affects the structure of production, it is clear that any alteration to the structure of interest rates will alter prevailing investment patterns. Maturity mismatching may breed instabilities much farther-reaching than fragility in the banking system. In combination with credit expansion,[6] maturity mismatching can breed malinvestment. As credit expansion improves the likelihood that loans taken today can be renewed in the future, an increased amount of short-term borrowing will be undertaken to fund longer-term loans. An ever-riskier situation is fostered whereby a pyramid of illiquid long-term loans may make the banking system insolvent should an event arise whereby the sustaining short-term loans cannot be renewed, a situation that has been called "sudden stop syndrome".[7] If the perception of risk increases, it becomes

---

Rothbard touches on maturity mismatching: "*Another way of looking at the essential and inherent unsoundness of fractional reserve banking is to note a crucial rule of sound financial management—one that is observed everywhere except in the banking business. Namely, that the time structure of the firm's assets should be no longer than the time structure of its liabilities.*" Murray N. Rothbard, *The Mystery of Banking*, Second edition (Auburn, Ala.: Ludwig von Mises Institute, 2008), p. 98.

[5]This procedure is more commonly referred to as borrowing short and lending long. A downside of this terminology is that demand deposits are erroneously considered as short-term borrowing, at least in the present fractional reserve banking system. Both economically and legally it is questionable whether these fractional reserve demand deposits can be viewed as loans (Jesús Huerta de Soto, *Money, Bank Credit, and Economic Cycles*, Second edition [Auburn, Ala.: Ludwig von Mises Institute, 2006], Philipp Bagus and David Howden, "the Legitimacy of Loan Maturity Mismatching: A Risky, but Not Fraudulent Undertaking," *The Journal of Business Ethics* 90, no. 3 [2009], pp. 399–406).

[6]For a detailed examination of the economics of maturity mismatching see Philipp Bagus, "Austrian Business Cycle Theory: Are 100 Percent Reserves Sufficient to Prevent a Business Cycle?" *Libertarian Papers* 2, No. 2 (2010). See Bagus and Howden, "The Legitimacy of Loan Maturity Mismatching," for the ethical aspects of this practice.

[7]Guillermo A. Calvo "Capital Flows and Capital-Market Crises: The Simple Economics of Sudden Stops," *Journal of Applied Economics* 1 (1998): pp. 35-54.

more likely that short-term loans will not be continued, creating an illiquid situation for those banks that find themselves with an unsustainably mismatched loan portfolio.

Today's banking system has made a curious change to earlier practice. Economists and bankers today disregard the golden rule, arguing that the very function of banking is to systematically violate it. For instance, Paul de Grauwe[8] regards banks as institutions "which inevitably borrow short and lend long," thus providing an "essential service."[9] Similarly, Douglas W. Diamond and Philip H. Dybvig[10] regard the transformation of illiquid claims (banks' assets) into liquid claims (demand deposits) as necessary.[11]

While the maturity mismatching is profitable and many modern economists endorse the practice, it carries the danger of insolvency. Thus, the question still remains: Why did Icelandic banks engage so heavily in this risky practice?

The answer is straightforward. Like banks in other countries,

---

[8]Paul de Grauwe, "Returning to Narrow Banking," in *What G20 Leaders Must Do to Stabilize Our Economy and Fix the Financial System*, ed. Barry Eichengreen and Richard Baldwin, pp. 37–39 (London: Centre for Economic Policy Research, 2008), p. 37.

[9]Interestingly, de Grauwe sees this leading to an "inherently fragile system," and advocates a return to a form of "narrow banking," with commercial banks prohibited from investing in derivatives and complex structured products. He does not see the restriction of maturity mismatching that a free market system would create. As banks would be fully accountable for their risky loan portfolios (i.e., they would not have government-enacted bailout guarantees or subsidized deposit insurance), maturity-mismatched portfolios would be strictly curtailed. Furthermore, in a free market there is no need for the government to prohibit negative working capital for private companies; companies avoid it out of caution. Similarly, in a free market there is no need to prohibit banks from mismatching maturities.

[10]Douglas W. Diamond and Philip H. Dybvig, "Bank Runs, Deposit Insurance, and Liquidity," *Journal of Political Economy* 91, No. 3 (1983): pp. 401–19.

[11]See also Tobias Adrian and Hyun Song Shin, "Financial Intermediaries, Financial Stability, and Monetary Policy," Paper presented at the Federal Reserve Bank of Kansas City Symposium at Jackson Hole (August 21–23, 2008), and Xavier Freixas and Jean-Charles Rochet, *Microeconomics of Banking*, Second edition (Cambridge, Mass.: MIT Press, 2008) for similar views.

Icelandic banks enjoyed guarantees by the government to bail them out should their bets on the market turn out to have been wrong. But while this guarantee is merely implicitly assumed in most developed economies, the Central Bank of Iceland had committed itself explicitly to providing this function.[12] At the critical point when liquidity was at risk of faltering, the CBI would function as the effective "roller-over" of last resort, providing fresh short-term debt as the market required it.

While this guarantee affected all Icelandic banks covered under the guarantee of the CBI, the three main banks, Kaupthing, Glitnir, and Landsbanki, had an additional perverse incentive. They were widely considered so big (with total assets almost eleven times the size of Iceland's 2007 GDP) that they could regard themselves as too big to fail. The authorities could be expected to fear that if one of the large banks failed it would take with it companies that had stakes in it, and these bankruptcies would negatively affect other banks that were financing them. The larger and more interwoven the Icelandic banking sector became, the higher the probability that a single bank would be considered too big to fail. If a large bank became insolvent, a bailout would be all but inevitable. The three large banks' sense that they were too big to fail created a moral hazard. With no fears of becoming insolvent should their bets on finding future short-term funding turn out to have been wrong, the Icelandic banking sector was granted a privilege to engage in exceedingly risky behavior. The Central Bank of Iceland had effectively given a green light to the banks to shoulder increasing amounts of short-term risk uncompensated by assets of corresponding risk or duration. This seemed to work well until global liquidity dried up following the collapse of the American bank Lehman Brothers in late 2008. With a sudden dearth of funding—especially wholesale short-term funding—Icelandic banks were unable to

---

[12]See Central Bank of Iceland, "New Act on the Central Bank of Iceland," Press Release (November 13, 2001), for the document that, among other things, promises a new era of price stability through an inflation-targeting framework, and the formal provision of a lender of last resort function.

roll over the debts that they had to roll over in order to remain solvent.

While the interbank loan market had dried up, removing the possibility of rolling over short-term debts, the banking system was also losing deposits. Depositors were beginning to get nervous about the prospects for the banks, especially after the failure of Glitnir on September 29, 2008. Small retailers were withdrawing funds, effectively failing to roll their deposits over. Banks in today's fractional reserve system treat deposits as loans of zero maturity. By loaning out against them, they rely on a continued "renewal" of these deposits to maintain solvency. Any withdrawal of deposits stops the rollover, bringing banks to a liquidity crunch. Kaupthing's subsidiary Kaupthing Edge was accustomed to net inflows of £100–150 million per week until mid-2008. In September 2008 this flow reversed to an *out*flow of £50 million per week. Deposits were leaking out and new depositors were difficult to attract.[13]

The explicit guarantee to bail out insolvent banks resulted in excessive maturity mismatching. Other central bank policies made the mismatching worse. On March 21, 2003, in a push to homogenize banking practices with the European Central Bank, the CBI reduced the reserve requirement for deposit institutions from four to two percent.[14] This change increased the money multiplier from eight times to fifteen times.[15] For liabilities maturing more than two years in the future, no allowance in reserves was required.

Unlike his counterparts at other countries' central banks, the Central Bank of Iceland's governor, Davíð Oddsson (the former Prime Minister), commensurately changed the reserve requirements that banks would have to safeguard in their vaults for

---

[13]Thorvaldsson, *Frozen Assets*, p. 209.

[14]Benjamin Hunt, Robert Tchaidze, and Ann-Margret Westin, "Iceland: Selected Issues," IMF country Report No. 05/366 (2005), p. 33.

[15]Ásgeir Jónsson, *Why Iceland? How One of the World's Smallest Countries Became the Meltdown's Biggest Casualty* (New York: McGraw Hill, 2009), p. 65.

a rainy day. By lowering this salient rate, the central bank allowed the banks to free up and use an additional portion of the deposits previously entrusted to them. A lower reserve ratio allows for a more pronounced credit expansion. Even without any increase in the supply of base money, decreasing the reserve requirement rate augments the credit supply immensely. As a result of the 2003 decision to lower reserve requirements, many banks needed to "park" their liquidity somewhere.[16] An excess of liquidity in the banking system worked its way quickly to the loans market. In particular, there was a massive influx of funds into the mortgage market as banks tried to loan out their newly superfluous reserves.

Like all entrepreneurs, bankers eagerly search out and exploit profit opportunities. One simple way for banks to make a profit is to take advantage of the funds entrusted to them by depositors for safekeeping and issue them to businesses as loans, thus earning a profit-generating interest rate spread. Fractional reserves on demand deposits allows for credit expansion. Credit expansion serves to create new deposits and thereby increase the money supply. Under the guarantee of generous bailouts by the CBI, Iceland's banks were more than willing to err against the side of prudence and always remain fully lent out, keeping reserve balances at the bare minimum legally necessary to satisfy their regulators. By lowering the reserve ratio repeatedly during the boom, the central bank allowed banks to issue increased credit against funds already deposited with them.

In 2003, at exactly the same time that it increased liquidity by reducing reserve requirements, the CBI commenced an extended period of lowering interest rates. In lowering its interest rates, Iceland was not the only culprit. The Federal Reserve lowered its borrowing rate by 5.5 percent during the boom, the European Central Bank lowered its rate 2.75 percent, and the Bank of Canada lowered its rate by 3.75 percent. Even the venerable Bank of England lowered its key rate by 2.5 percent. But

---

[16] Hunt, Tchaidze, and Westin, "Iceland: Selected Issues," p. 33 n. 8.

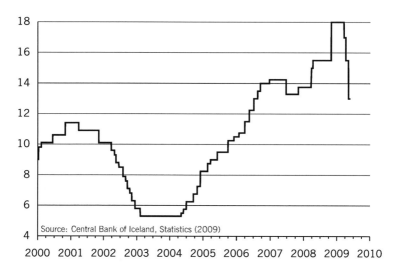

Figure 1: Central Bank of Iceland policy rate (percent)

in Iceland, unlike in many other developed economies, fresh credit issued via the artificially lowered central bank lending rates was not the only cause of the credit-fueled boom; Iceland further stimulated the expansion of credit by also lowering the reserve requirement ratio. (By way of comparison, during the 2000s while the Central Bank of Iceland was lowering its reserve requirement, America's Federal Reserve kept its own reserve requirement for demand deposits steady at ten percent.) The lowering of interest rates and the reduction of the reserve requirement together ensured that the Iceland boom reached manic heights unreachable without the encouragement of ample credit, heights which other central banks of the world aspired to reach, but could not owing their own policy limitations.

When the Central Bank of Iceland shifted to a flexible exchange rate for the króna on March 27, 2001 it also adopted an inflation targeting framework for monetary policy. This change was widely heralded at the time, with promises that it would place the Central Bank of Iceland in a better position to integrate Iceland's economy into the growing world economy, as well as effectively rein in inflation.[17] By shedding the constraints of its fixed exchange rate regime and taking full control of its monetary policy the CBI hoped to bring a responsible era of low and stable inflation.

For most of Iceland's recent history, inflation had been high and volatile. With this in mind, the Central Bank of Iceland targeted 2.5 percent price inflation, and set the margin of error at plus or minus 1.5 percent, both a higher base rate and a wider acceptable range than most central banks.[18] When the inflation rate nevertheless breached the tolerance band beginning in February 2005, the question that arose in many peoples' minds was "How tightly is it feasible to control inflation in Iceland?"[19]

From its inception, the CBI's targeting scheme gave some commentators cause for concern. Iceland's history of inflation volatility, mostly in tune with the season's catch of fish, was a critical difficulty. Cautioning against the lofty goal of controlling Iceland's inflation, Frank Engles[20] remarked that effective inflation-targeting frameworks are "crucially dependent" on the central bank's ability to accurately predict inflation.

Within the CBI's targeting model lay the concealed assumption of a constant exchange rate over the forecast horizon.[21] Starting in the second half of 2001, this assumption proved to be the model's Achilles heel. As the króna exchange rate started to strengthen, the model persistently underestimated the inflation rate.[22] Consequently, increases in the money supply were greater than would have been optimal given the inflation target. Strong increases in the money supply, in turn, drove interest

---

[17]See, for example, Eduardo Aninat, "IMF Welcomes Flotation of Iceland's Króna," *IMF News Brief* No. 01/29, (March 28, 2001).

[18]Keiko Honjo and Benjamin Hunt, "Stabilizing Inflation in Iceland," IMF Working Paper WP/06/262 (2006), p. 3.

[19]Hunt, Tchaidze, and Westin, "Iceland: Selected Issues," p. 3.

[20]Frank Engles, "Iceland: Selected Issues and Statistical Appendix," IMF Country Report no. 01/82 (2001), p. 3.

[21]Engles, "Iceland."

[22]Frank Engles and Michael Gapen, "Iceland: Selected Issues," IMF Country Report no. 02/129 (2002), pp. 8–9.

rates on loans lower than they should prudently have been allowed to go if the inflation target was to be attained.

The root of this extremely accommodating monetary policy can be found within the efficient monetary policy frontier model employed by the CBI. The model, which estimated the locus of inflation and output gap alternatives given distinct policy choices, rested on four main factors: the output gap, expected inflation, expected foreign exchange rate, and monetary policy reaction function. These parameters were all forecast using Bayesian estimations; prior distributions of these variables were combined with current data in an attempt to estimate the posterior parameter distributions. Using prior data would prove to have been a poor choice. Iceland had a relatively short experience with its new flexible exchange rate regime; as a result, the data set encompassed two different policy regimes, so it provided estimates that were not wholly applicable.[23]

While the data for the model were taken from a previous and non-applicable exchange rate regime, the distributions themselves were taken from a similar policy model employed by the Bank of Canada, and were then fine-tuned with minor adjustments, explored in Pétursson.[24] For example, Canada's model estimated the target interest rate for an open economy using the United States as the relevant foreign sector. Iceland modified this by substituting the euro area, the United States, and the United Kingdom as the foreign sectors. But while Canada shares many policy inputs with its neighbor and largest trading partner, there are few such similarities between Iceland and the three economies used in the model as its foreign sector participants. Canada's interest rates are highly correlated with America's, as are its capital flows (since the two nations are each other's primary trading partner). Iceland's interest rates are controlled by much different factors than its European (or

---

[23] Hunt, Tchaidze, and Westin, "Iceland: Selected Issues," p. 11.

[24] Thórarinn G. Pétursson, "Wage and Price Formation in a Small Open Economy: Evidence from Iceland," Central Bank of Iceland Working Paper no. 16 (2002).

American) counterparts'; capital flows are influenced by a myriad of factors not amenable to inclusion in the inflation targeting framework borrowed from the Bank of Canada.

Perhaps the most troubling aspect of using a borrowed inflation-targeting framework is that Iceland's inflation band was so much wider than most other countries'. In particular, it was four times as wide as the inflation band of Canada, the country from which the Central Bank of Iceland borrowed its model. One remedy that the CBI used was to exclude several volatile inputs from its inflation factor. This smoothed the data, making the foreign targeting model easier to implement. Housing, energy, and food were inputs that the CBI excluded from the consumer price index (CPI) because they normally suffered much variability in price.[25]

However much excluding these inputs may have increased the model's usability, it brought at least two serious problems at the same time.[26] First, nearly all of Iceland's food is imported, making food an essential component of any inflation computation. Second, energy prices were extremely volatile over the forecast period, affecting not only real inflation but also inflationary expectations. Iceland's "dated exchange rate targeting framework" was not able to cope with the massive changes that had occurred in the economy over its recent history.[27] Cheap credit flowed into several key areas of the economy, primarily

---

[25] Officially measured CPI inflation allocates housing costs twenty percent of the index—higher than any other European nation. The sharp increases in housing prices caused large divergences between actual and CBI-computed inflation rates. In July 2005, for example, 12-month actual inflation measured 3.5 percent, but with the housing component excluded, inflation would only have registered a 0.1 percent increase over the same period (Hunt, Tchaidze, and Westin, "Iceland: Selected Issues," p. 38).

[26] Hunt, Tchaidze, and Westin, "Iceland: Selected Issues."

[27] Paul Kupiec, "Iceland: Financial System Stability Assessment Update, including Report on the Observance and Standards and Codes on the following topics: Banking Supervision, Insurance Regulation, Securities Regulation, Payment Systems, and Monetary and Financial Policy Transparency," IMF Country Report no. 03/271 (2003).

household spending and power-intensive industries, adding to inflationary pressures. The rapid growth in domestic demand put pressure on the prices of the relatively fixed supply of goods the island had available. This imbalance maintained upward pressure on inflation, causing it to stay well above the central bank's target rate throughout the mid-2000s.[28]

These problems were noted relatively early in Iceland's boom. Honjo and Hunt[29] and Keiko Honjo and Srobona Mitra[30] both recommended abandoning the efficient monetary frontier framework and implementing a simpler fiscal rule in its place. These economists cited the volatility of price inflation as the prime reason for the model's lack of usability, though it should be noted that, given the parameters that were used, even stable inflation would have underestimated policy interest rates.

Moreover, there is no way to measure price inflation objectively in the first place. Comprised of an aggregate average of prices in the economy, any measured inflation rate is arbitrary. There is a plethora of different and changing prices in the economy. Which ones should be selected? The selection of goods in the basket is arbitrary, the weighting of the different prices is arbitrary, corrections to factor for qualitative improvements are arbitrary, and changes in the composition and the method of calculating the average are arbitrary. Every individual faces a unique inflation rate owing to his or her personal spending pattern. Any measured inflation rate will consequently diverge from the inflation rate facing any individual investor or entrepreneur.

These flaws acted in concert to underestimate present price inflation and allow for a looser monetary policy than was warranted given Iceland's targeting framework. An International Monetary Fund staff visit to the country in 2004 warned that short-term interest rates should be increased quickly to com-

---

[28] International Monetary Fund, "Iceland—2004 Staff Visit Concluding Statement," (October 25, 2004).

[29] Honjo and Hunt, "Stabilizing Inflation."

[30] Keiko Honjo and Srobona Mitra, "Iceland: Selected Issues," IMF country Report no. 06/297 (2006).

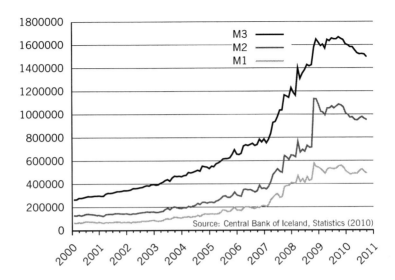

**Figure 2:** Icelandic money supply (January 2000–October 2010, million krónur)[31]

pensate for these too-low rates.[32] Imbalances were identified, leading to a widely held view that an adjustment process was necessary and that it would be better to get it over with sooner rather than later. For almost ten years following the return to a flexible exchange rate regime, both actual inflation and future inflationary expectations were continually underestimated, and as a consequence the market was flooded with an ever increasing supply of money.

This extremely accommodating monetary policy, both domestically and internationally, made ample quantities of liquidity available to be borrowed and invested. The money supply grew at a steady pace until late 2005. At this point an inflationary trend surged as the CBI steadily opened the monetary spigots (Figure 2). Broad-based money and credit aggregates

---

[31]Icelandic M1 is defined as all demand deposits plus currency in circulation. M2 includes M1 plus sight deposits. M3 adds time deposits to the M2 figure to derive the broadest money supply measure.

[32]IMF, "2004 Staff Visit."

|      | M3 | M2 | M1 |
|------|----|----|----|
| 2000 | 11 | −3 | 4  |
| 2001 | 17 | 12 | 6  |
| 2002 | 13 | 9  | 12 |
| 2003 | 21 | 27 | 43 |
| 2004 | 17 | 23 | 24 |
| 2005 | 18 | 22 | 22 |
| 2006 | 15 | 20 | 17 |
| 2007 | 57 | 82 | 100|
| 2008 | 34 | 59 | 29 |
| 2009 | 0  | −3 | −6 |
| 2010[34] | −6 | −4 | −1 |

Source: Central Bank of Iceland, Statistics (2010)

**Table 2**: Icelandic money supply growth (percent)

such as M2 grew at a rate over twenty percent *per annum every year between 2003 and 2008* (Table 2).[33] By the peak of the frenzy in 2008, M1 (the monetary base) had grown almost 500 percent on its level at the turn of the 21$^{st}$ century.

While the economy was likewise growing substantially, it was not enough to stave off the inflationary pressures created by such an expansion. Consumer price inflation rose above five percent for much of the Iceland boom's duration. Real interest rates were driven lower as a result, giving the island's small population an incentive to start spending rather than watch the value of their savings decline in an account. This increased demand for goods further served to mount inflationary pressures on the economy, thus spurring further spending. There was another, and arguably more direct, effect from the sharp growth in the money supply that the central bank had undertaken.

The Central Bank of Iceland's continual credit creation policy drove short-term interest rates substantially lower than they

---

[33]M1 includes all notes and coins in circulation, plus demand deposits (overdraft limits included).

would have been without this excess liquidity. Consequently, individuals had a strong incentive to borrow for the short-term at these artificially low rates. Starting in the early 2000s, approximately half of all Icelandic borrowing was undertaken on adjustable rates in order to take advantage of low short-term rates that were expected to remain reasonably low for the foreseeable future. Thórarinn G. Pétursson[35] estimates that the CBI had de facto control of the yield curve for loan maturities of up to twelve months.

Usually central banks are constrained somewhat in their monetary policy options as they control only the short-term rates. The dominant role of long-term bonds provides a brake on long-term monetary policy, as central banks do not typically engage in commensurate long-term lending. But maturity mismatching translates artificially low short-term rates into artificially low long-term rates since banks increase the supply of long-term funds by lending long.

In addition to this process driving long-term rates lower, there was another state agency besides the CBI ready to ensure that long-term rates remained artificially reduced, enabling ample amounts of borrowing to continue pushing the economy into an unsustainable boom. The government created the Housing Financing Fund (HFF) in 1999 to take over the role and assets of its predecessor, the State Housing Board. The HFF provided mortgage loans. Private dwellings became the focal point of its operations, although companies and non-governmental agencies could also make use of its services. The HFF took the mortgage market by storm. By mid-2004 almost 90 percent of Icelandic households held an HFF loan, and HFF-issued bonds comprised more than half of the Icelandic bond market.[36] Thus, not only were short-term interest rates manipulated and unduly

---

[34] Year to date, October 1, 2010.

[35] Thórarinn G. Pétursson, "The Transmission Mechanism of Monetary Policy: Analyzing the Financial Market Pass-Through," Central Bank of Iceland Working Paper no. 14 (2001).

[36] Hunt, Tchaidze and Westin, "Iceland: Selected Issues," p. 29.

lowered via a politically entrenched central bank, the long-term rates were likewise reduced via the government-controlled Housing Financing Fund. During the period leading to the financial crisis, the people of other countries saw a direct reduction only in their short-term interest rates, as a result of the policies of their central banks, but the people of Iceland were misled at all maturities of the yield curve.

The result of these policies was the extreme maturity mismatching that would eventually crash Iceland's economy. Nowhere was the maturity mismatch as pronounced as in the three largest Icelandic banks, Kaupthing, Glitnir and Landsbanki. Figure 3 shows the maturity mismatch just prior to the breakdown of the financial system in late 2008. The funding gaps (i.e., liabilities minus assets for different maturities) of these banks as they issued short-term liabilities in order to invest in long-term assets are shown to be most severe for the most short-term (i.e., most liquid) securities.[37] The three-month funding gap of 623 billion krónur amounted to almost fifty percent of the 2007 Icelandic GDP (1,279 billion krónur). In other words, the Icelandic economy as a whole would have needed half a year to cover the three-month funding gap that would result from a full roll-over stop.

What are the economic effects of maturity mismatching? The most obvious effect is that it can make the banking system unstable. If liquidity declines too much, lenders do not renew short-term debt, and a maturity-mismatched bank becomes illiquid. The problem can then spread quickly to the whole financial system. Illiquid banks are forced to sell assets to cover their funding shortfalls, and this selling depresses asset prices. As asset prices collapse, banks have to write down capital, and they

---

[37] These three largest banks dominated the Icelandic financial landscape, with assets which ballooned to 1100 percent of Icelandic GDP in 2007 (Willem H. Buiter and Anne Sibert, "The Icelandic Banking Crisis and What to Do About it: The Lender of Last Resort Theory of Optimal Currency Areas," *Centre for Economic Policy Research Policy Insight* no. 26 (October, 2008): p. 4) and comprised nearly eighty percent of total Icelandic banking assets.

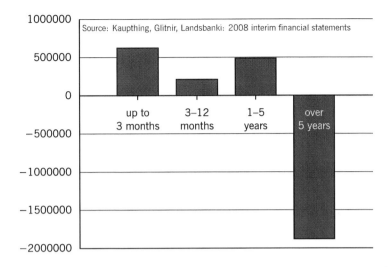

**Figure 3**: Funding gap: big three banks (as at June 2008, in million krónur)[38]

face insolvency. This may induce other market participants to stop rolling over loans to banks, leading to a panic or, worse, a credit freeze. Trust in the banking system quickly evaporates. Liquidity problems spread and banks liquidate further assets to cover growing losses. During a panic, the long-term assets can only be sold at a significant loss, and so bank losses are increased. A bank run may ensue, leading to further liquidations and price declines. The whole banking system may eventually collapse.

Hence, any rumor of problems concerning bank solvency can cause a rollover stoppage and thereby the breakdown of the financial system.

As recently as September 2007, the British retail bank Northern Rock had failed. As housing prices and mortgage-backed securities started to decline in value, wholesale short-term fund-

---

[38] The funding gap presents the liabilities less assets of a certain maturity. A positive funding gap of maturities up to three months means that there are more liabilities coming due in this period than there are assets maturing.

ing backed by these assets dried up. Depositors made an old-fashioned run on the bank that would have made *It's a Wonderful Life*'s Henry Potter proud.[39]

Another crucial effect of an excessive level of maturity-mismatched loans is that it creates distortions in the real economy. It distorts the capital structure, as demonstrated by Austrian business cycle theory. Demand deposits are bank liabilities that are due immediately (i.e., they have zero maturity). Because demand deposits are used to finance long-term investment projects, credit expansion contains extreme maturity mismatching. A similar maturity mismatch occurred when Icelandic banks borrowed in (mainly international) wholesale markets, via short-term interbank loans and repurchase agreements, asset-backed commercial paper, etc., in order to invest in long-term loans, such as commercial and residential mortgages.[40]

The ultimate problem with maturity mismatching is that there are insufficient savings available to complete the artificially high number of projects undertaken. Take a typical mortgage, for example. Lenders have only saved for three months (the term of the commercial paper) or they have not saved at all (the term of the deposit); in any case they have not saved for thirty or forty years, which is the term of the

---

[39]Hyun Song Shin, "Reflections on Northern Rock: The Bank Run That Heralded the Global Financial Crisis," *Journal of Economic Perspectives* 23, no. 1 (2009): pp. 101–19, assesses Northern Rock's crisis and treats it as an unconventional bank run, in which the bank's evaporating long-term asset base could not fund its short-term liabilities.

[40]There exist, however, important differences between credit expansion and other types of maturity mismatching—credit expansion increases the money supply (Bagus, "Austrian Business Cycle Theory"). Furthermore, an initially created unbacked demand deposit may lead to a far greater expansion of demand deposits if the rest of the banking system follows suit. Other types of maturity mismatching do not increase the money supply. Another difference lies in the ethical status of the practices. Credit expansion can be regarded as fraudulent, while borrowing short and lending long (i.e., maturity mismatching) is risky but not fraudulent (Bagus and Howden, "The Legitimacy of Loan Maturity Mismatching").

mortgage. Maturity mismatching deceives both investors and entrepreneurs about the available supply of long-term savings. By borrowing short and lending long, banks cause an artificial reduction of long-term interest rates. Entrepreneurs think that more long-term savings are available than really exist, and so they engage in malinvestments, which will have to be liquidated once it becomes obvious that there are not enough *real* savings to sustain them.

Interestingly, the maturity mismatch completes the skewing of the interest rate yield curve that the central bank commences but is usually unable to complete on its own. Central bank open-market operations are typically limited to the short end of the yield curve. Because central banks control their discount rate by offering short-term loans, typically thirty days or less, they are able to manipulate only these extremely short-term rates. The banking system transforms these artificial low short-term rates into artificial low long-term rates through maturity mismatching. By borrowing short, banks create an additional demand for short-term funds, thus bidding up short-term rates. By lending long, they create an additional supply of long-term funding, thus causing a decline of long-term rates. Thus, maturity mismatching flattens the yield curve, and transfers the effect of central bank manipulation of short-term rates to the long-term end of the curve.[41]

In Chapter 5 we will analyze specific malinvestments committed by the Icelandic financial system due to the increase in credit by the Central Bank of Iceland. But before we turn to this subject, we will explain the factor that potentiated the effects of maturity mismatching.

---

[41]Philipp Bagus and David Howden, "The Term Structure of Savings, the Yield Curve, and Maturity Mismatching," *Quarterly Journal of Austrian Economics* 13, no. 3 (2010): pp. 64–85.

Chapter 3

# The IMF, Moral Hazard, and the Temptation of Foreign Funds

The late 1990s saw a strengthening of the International Monetary Fund's core mandate as a global financial parent, on the lookout for perceived instabilities to correct in the name of economic development. Several alterations in the scope of its operations following the crises of the previous twenty years had given the Fund a far wider range of policy options, as well as far greater resources, with which to support faltering economies.

The crises of the late 1980s and '90s—the Mexican peso crisis, the Russian debt default, the Asian crisis, the Brazilian currency crisis, and the Argentine crisis, among others—all were used to strengthen the Fund's core operating mandate, which is to stabilize exchange rates in order to facilitate global trade. The IMF's failures to immediately stabilize previous crises were reckoned to have been due to a lack of procedural guidelines allowing it to speedily aid the ailing economies. Each time a shortcoming appeared following the IMF's rush to maintain global financial stability, it was assumed that the existing scope of operations was inadequate, not that there was something fundamentally wrong with the very existence of these operations.

In some ways, Iceland's financial crisis could be recorded in the history books as much like the crises in Mexico, Russia, Brazil, Argentina, or any number of Asian nations. However, it differs in two major ways. First, the extent of its boom and subsequent collapse are much greater than anything experienced in the aforementioned developing countries. More important, and more puzzling, is the fact that Iceland is the first *developed* country to suffer a financial calamity of this scope since the Great Depression.

In response to these prior financial collapses, the world's centralized banking and monetary authorities, headed primarily by the International Monetary Fund, collaborated to initiate a period of surveillance, aid, and guarantees for the world's financial markets the extent of which had never been seen before. The short-term result was a long period of expansion and calm. Capital markets remained eerily liquid, even in the wake of such traumatic events as the September 11 attacks. The foreign exchange markets entered a period of reduced volatility. Investor optimism not only increased accordingly, it turned into irrational exuberance (to borrow a well-known phrase). The result of this artificially induced calm was a general underpricing of uncertainty. It is now widely recognized that the overleveraged banking system was unsustainable.

When seeking an explanation for this reduced perception of risk and for the rapid growth in cross-border investments, it seems reasonable to start by looking at currency markets, since money is the link between all transactions. But foreign exchange rates have not entered a period of what we could consider unusual calm, nor has our ability to forecast these rates improved significantly.[1] If anything, (with the exception

---

[1] Richard A. Meese and Kenneth Rogoff, "Empirical Exchange Rate Models of the Seventies: Do They Fit Out of Sample?" *Journal of International Economics* 14 (1983): pp. 3–24, and Richard A. Meese, "Currency Fluctuations in the Post-Bretton Woods Era," *Journal of Economic Perspectives* 4, no. 1

of the expanding European Monetary Zone) the tendency has been for additional countries to switch to floating exchange-rate regimes. This has made an additional component of entrepreneurial foresight necessary to navigate the market. Not only must input costs and output prices be estimated, but if either side of the profit equation is reckoned in a currency different from one's own, the exchange rate fluctuation during the intervening period must also be approximated.

If the average risk of cross-border investing has not been reduced, specific volatile episodes have been greatly mitigated. International organizations have been only too eager to step in to prevent sovereign bankruptcies, those cases where governments declare bankruptcy, typically by defaulting on their debts and inflating their currency to worthlessness. The IMF has progressed through a period of increasing interventions into small or developing economies, aimed at saving investors from undue volatility or losses.

Following the Asian crises of the late 1990s, the IMF embarked upon an unprecedented expansion of its operating powers. The Fund disbursed deals worth $17 billion for Thailand, $43 billion for Indonesia, and $57 billion for South Korea—deals with conditions stretching far beyond the IMF's operating mandate.[2] Of course, the IMF was not only battling economic crises in exotic locales, but also a political crisis closer to home. The Fund, which was formed in 1944 as part of the Bretton Woods Standard, had suffered a loss of relevance due to recent changes in the international monetary system. The Fund originally had four goals: 1) promotion of exchange rate stability, 2) cooperation of monetary policy, 3) expansion of international trade, and 4) to function as a lender of last resort. In the early days of Bretton Woods, with a complex array of fixed exchange rates, at least some of these goals could not be promoted by individual countries. Constrained by their

---

(1990): pp. 117–134, provide evidence that the predictive value that economic models have for monthly or quarterly exchange rates is essentially zero.

[2]Devesh Kapur, "The IMF: A Cure or a Curse?" *Foreign Policy* 111 (Summer, 1998): pp. 114–129.

respective exchange rate regimes, many countries found their interventionist hands tied when crises developed.

A shift to a global system of flexible-rate monetary regimes altered the situation fundamentally. Central banks could unilaterally expand their monetary base to combat liquidity crises, irrespective of depreciations of exchange rates (which had been constrained under the previous Bretton Woods system). There was no need to explicitly coordinate cross-border monetary policies. Each country's central bank could pursue its own policy, for better or worse, and reap the benefits or shoulder the costs of its own decisions. International trade was hardly in need of further promotion. The vast majority of the world had witnessed the advantages that open borders had created during the post war period, and physical barriers to trade were becoming a thing of the past. A panoply of acronymed trade agreements, both unilateral and bilateral, appeared which promoted free trade without the need for an international bureaucracy like the International Monetary Fund.

These changes led to a crisis of relevance for the IMF. Effectively, it was left with only one of its four original goals to pursue: maintaining the stability of exchange rates. Admittedly, with the new and ever expanding complex of flexible rates, this could be viewed as being a broader goal than ever before. The prevalence of flexible rates also gave the Fund an excuse to begin intervening at the slightest whiff of trouble to ensure that exchange rates remained "stable," or "controlled," lest the now-secondary goal of promoting international trade be threatened.

Indeed, calls for increasing regulation over monetary affairs were becoming the norm. The IMF was changing from a reactive agency to aid those only *after* they required help and had exhausted all other options, to a proactive agency intruding in others' affairs before a need was even apparent.[3] Following the Latin American and, especially, the South-East Asian crises of the 1990s, the calls for regulation intensified.

---

[3] Effectively, the Fund had become a "lender of first resort" (Daniel Cohen and Richard Portes, "Toward a Lender of First Resort," International Monetary Fund working paper WP/06/66, 2009).

"Governments must now preside over a process of strengthening the institutional and policy bases of their economies to make them hardy enough to withstand and the benefit from globalization.... The IMF can and should play a role in advancing every part of this process," declared David Lipton.[4] While discussing the financial role of the IMF, "[t]he important point", according to Jack Boorman,[5] was that "liberalization and privatization do not imply a lesser role for government.... If the crisis has taught us anything, it should be a reminder of the key importance of the *institutional* infrastructure needed to manage a successful market capitalist economy—legal systems, bankruptcy procedures, standards, transparency—many of the things now captured under the heading of architecture." The IMF's Deputy Managing Director, Anne Krueger, reiterated these sentiments to the Icelandic public at a speech given on June 24, 2004 at the Central Bank of Iceland:

> Crises have always been part of the Fund's work. The challenge for the IMF is to do as much as possible to prevent them, but, once crises occur, to resolve them as smoothly as possible.[6]

As the current crisis worsened a large number of government deficits, the Fund has called on the world's developing countries to make more resources available for it to combat the crisis. At a recent summit, the G20 agreed to *triple* the IMF's lending capability to $750 billion.[7] It pledged to expand the

---

[4] David Lipton, "Refocusing the Role of the International Monetary Fund," in *Reforming the International Monetary System*, eds. Peter B. Kenen and Alexander K. Swoboda, pp. 345–365 (Washington, D.C.: International Monetary Fund, 2000), p. 346.

[5] Jack Boorman, "On the Financial Role of the IMF," in *Reforming the International Monetary System*, eds. Peter B. Kenen and Alexander K. Swoboda, pp. 366–369 (Washington, D.C.: International Monetary Fund, 2000), p. 366.

[6] Anne Krueger, "The IMF at Sixty: What Role for the Future?" Lecture at the Central Bank of Iceland, Reykjavik (June 24, 2004).

[7] It is no longer clear whether the IMF will get what was originally promised to it. Only about half of this amount has been firmly pledged by governments to date.

IMF's own "currency" unit, the special drawing right, by $250 billion.[8]

As rapid and substantial support is given to countries at risk of liquidity or solvency problems, foreign investors' confidence remains elevated and their fear of default is removed (or at least reduced). They are enticed to take on higher degrees of debt in these countries. The elevated level of investment in these countries results in increased instability.

A second danger also arises from enhancing the stability of a country's finances. As international investment and confidence

---

[8]Some have suggested that an international institution, such as the International Monetary Fund (IMF), should function as an international lender of last resort (Stanley Fischer, "On the Need for an International Lender of Last Resort," *Journal of Economic Perspectives* 13 [1999]: pp. 85–104; Nouriel Roubini and Brad Setser, *Bailouts or Bail-Ins? Responding to Financial Crises in Emerging Economies* [Washington, D.C.: Institute for International Economics, 2004]; Maurice Obstfeld, "Lenders of Last Resort in a Globalized World," Keynote address, International Conference of the Institute for Monetary and Economic Studies, Tokyo, Bank of Japan [May 27–28, 2009]). Forrest Capie, "Can There Be an International Lender-of-Last-Resort?" *International Finance* 1, no. 2 (1998): pp. 311–325, and Jeffrey A. Frankel, "International Lender of Last Resort," Presented at the Federal Reserve Bank of Boston Conference "Rethinking the International Monetary System," (June 7–9, 1999), point out that the IMF *can't* function as a lender of last resort in the traditional sense, as it lacks the ability to print money. The fund, however, closely approximates this role given its large reserves relative to the size of the economies it aims at aiding. Michele Fratianni and John Pattison, "The Bank for International Settlements: An Assessment of Its Role in International Monetary and Financial Policy Coordination," *Open Economies Review* 12, no. 2 (2001): pp. 197–222, argue that the Bank of International Settlements should undertake the international role of a lender of last resort, while Varadarajan V. Chari and Patrick Kehoe, "Asking the Right Questions About the IMF," *Federal Reserve Bank of Minneapolis, Annual Report* (1999): pp. 3–26, claim that a consortium of the Fed, ECB and Bank of Japan would be large enough to combat international liquidity crises. Alternatively, Barry Eichengreen and Christof Rühl, "the Bail-In Problem: Systematic Goals, Ad Hoc Means," *Economic Systems* 25, no. 1 (2001): pp. 3–32, consider the role of collective-action provisions in loan agreements in helping determine when restructuring is desirable. Barry Eichengreen, *Toward a New International Financial Architecture: A Practical Post-Asia Agenda* (Washington, D.C.:

## The IMF, Moral Hazard, and the Temptation of Foreign Funds 33

in a country's long-term perspective are increased, the volatility of foreign exchanges rates is commensurately reduced.[9] Consequently, the enhanced financial stability gives domestic investors the advantage of denominating debts in foreign currencies, which often offer lower interest rates. This enables them to secure substantial savings as compared to using comparable financing denominated in the domestic currency. This shift from domestic to foreign sources of funding entails a cost that may or may not be embedded in the cost of borrowing; namely, the currency exchange risk inherent in any debt undertaking where the currency of the income source or asset is different from that of the liability.

Recently, the International Monetary Fund has stepped in to provide rules for insolvency reorganizations. In response to a number of major global financial crises throughout the 1990s, the IMF increased its role as an intermediary in these international affairs. There were increased calls for the IMF to function as an international lender of last resort in order to stave off these insolvency crises and allow for more orderly exits to normalcy.[10] With the existence of an overseeing agency, international capital markets could function with renewed confidence that future financial crises would not jeopardize debt repayments.

What is overlooked in this push for an international lender of last resort is that the more countries the IMF bails out, the

---

Institute for International Economics, 1999) surveys the relevant proposals.

[9]This risk reduction as it will affect the marginal lenders. Interest rates may stay at what appears to be a high level that fully compensates for the perceived risk, while at the same time enticing marginal lenders to shoulder more risk than they would like to at the going interest rate. Ludwig von Mises, "'Elastic Expectations' and the Austrian Theory of the Trade Cycle," *Economica*, n.s., 10, no. 39 (1943): pp. 251–52) pointed out that artificially depressed interest rates need not be low by any objective standard to have detrimental effects. Relative reductions compared to the real (i.e., not artificially manipulated) rate are sufficient to induce entrepreneurial error.

[10]Robert Gilpin, *The Challenge of Global Capitalism: The World Economy in the Twenty-First Century* (Princeton, N.J.: Princeton University Press, 2000), p. 335.

greater will be the moral hazard problem in other countries. In normal markets, lenders make loans to borrowers, and borrowers may enter bankruptcy. The debts are settled via a bankruptcy procedure in the court system; "this is how market economies are supposed to work."[11] Risky countries, and, more importantly, their creditors, view the guarantee of bailouts as an insurance policy. Investors are less cautious about investing in developing economies as the IMF has implicitly guaranteed to cover their losses in the event of a financial calamity.

The work to establish an international lender of last resort may be unnecessary in most instances. After all, a sovereign nation has the built-in advantage that its central bank can inflate the money supply and retire debt obligations denominated in its own currency.[12] This salient feature—a central bank acting as a lender of last resort—should eliminate the possibility that the banking system will become insolvent, provided debts are denominated in the domestic currency.

However, artificially induced stability in emerging countries has enabled entrepreneurs to diversify funding away from the domestic currency (which will still suffer from an embedded and elevated risk premium) and into more stable foreign currencies.[13] These foreign funding sources offer the advantage of a lower risk premium, which reduces the carrying cost of debt. Stable exchange rates induced by the IMF lead to an

---

[11]Joseph E. Stiglitz, *Globalization and Its Discontents* (New York: W. W. Norton and Company, 2003), p. 201.

[12]There are dollarized nations such as Monaco, Kosovo or Liechtenstein that have adopted foreign currencies, such as Euros or Swiss Francs. They lack the ability to inflate their debt obligations away (indeed, in some cases, there is actually no need for it: The Principality of Liechtenstein does not have any government debt). These are, however, in the minority compared to the number of sovereign nations with central banks and independent monetary policies.

[13]The International Monetary Fund ("Review of Recent Crisis Programs," [September 14, 2009], p. 45) has recently made note of this, stating that while exchange-rate stability is vital for the growth of developing economies, this goal must be framed against the potential future needs for adjustment.

underpricing of risk, in the form of decreased foreign exchange rate volatility. As a result, there are strong forces enticing both governments and entrepreneurs to take on liabilities in foreign currencies.

This underpricing of risk led Icelandic banks to take on liabilities denominated in foreign currency. It also caused an increase in international speculation in Iceland as foreigners were lulled into thinking the króna was less risky than its fundamentals would have suggested.

# Chapter 4

# Currency Mismatching

Domestic funds for profitable maturity mismatching were limited in Iceland's small economy. During the boom in the financial sector, banks started to look elsewhere for funds. Domestic retail deposits were very limited and did not satisfy the banks' lust for expansion, so they followed the path of U.S. investment banks that had no retail deposits at all: they used wholesale markets to fund their balance sheets and attract investment banking fees. Icelandic banks were able to tap these funds due to their strong credit ratings.

In 2003 Kaupthing merged with Bunadarbanki, and the combined bank received an A2 credit ranking, which drastically altered the way that the bank was funded. Now Kaupthing could issue bonds in international markets.[1] Kaupthing followed this strategy of buying better-rated banks to improve its own rating. The other Icelandic banks also improved their ratings during the global liquidity boom of the early 2000s, gaining access to international wholesale markets. Later on, Icelandic banks tried

---

[1] Thorvaldsson, *Frozen Assets*, p. 106.

to get further access to foreign retail markets by offering deposit accounts, mostly over the internet, to customers in Great Britain, the Netherlands, and Germany.

Thus, Icelandic banks borrowed foreign short-term funds to invest them for the long term, both domestically and internationally. This was especially attractive as domestic interest rates were higher than those of foreign central banks, which had undertaken even more extreme loose-money policies than the Central Bank of Iceland. This brings us to Iceland's second and more specific problem: currency mismatching.

Like maturity mismatching, currency mismatching is based on a profitable arbitrage, this time in exchange rates. While maturity mismatching makes use of the fact that interest rates normally are lower for shorter maturities than for longer maturities (variation of rates over time), currency mismatching exploits the differences between interest rates in different economies (variation of rates over space). Currency mismatching implies that investors indebt themselves in currency areas where interest rates are low and invest in countries where interest rates are high, the now-famous carry trade. Figure 4 depicts the substantial interest rate differences between the policy rates of the Fed, the ECB, and the Bank of Japan (BoJ) in comparison to the CBI.

As Icelandic interest rates were relatively high, investors indebted themselves in dollars, euros and yen at low interest rates and invested the proceeds in Icelandic assets. Like maturity mismatching, this is risky. When the currency that has been invested depreciates relative to the currency that is loaned, there may be considerable losses, resulting in the insolvency of the investors exploiting the carry trade.

As with maturity mismatching, the question that comes to mind about currency mismatching is why did Icelandic banks engage so heavily in this risky practice? And for that matter, why does anyone? The answer relates to implicit government guarantees. Because of implicit government guarantees, especially the possibility of obtaining IMF assistance in dire circumstances, people start to believe that exchange rate risk is reduced.

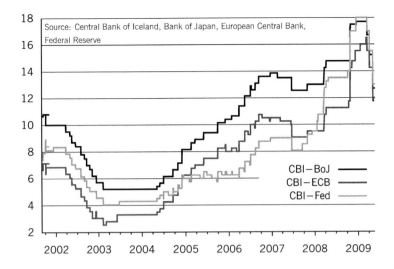

**Figure 4:** Interest rate gap of the CBI to the BoJ, ECB and the Fed (in percent)[2]

We may speak of an illusion caused by government guarantees. The illusion consists of the notion that government intervention can and will keep exchange rates more stable than is really the case.[3] If these actions artificially stabilize exchange rates, investors see less risk in the relatively profitable carry trade. The risk of losses from adverse exchange rate movements usually limits the extent of this practice. Entrepreneurs are alert to this risk; indeed, it is one of the fundamental concerns of internationally operating firms. For such firms, the currency of revenue may rarely coincide with the currency of expenses, so

---

[2]We used as interest rates the policy rate of the CBI, the federal funds target rate of the Fed, the Basic Discount Rate of the BoJ and the rate for the main refinancing operations of the ECB.

[3]Our point about the illusion of a stable fiat exchange rate is in line with Jörg Guido Hülsmann's ("Toward a General Theory of Error Cycles," *Quarterly Journal of Austrian Economics* 1, no. 4 [1998]: pp. 1–23) argument that government action provokes illusions that cause error cycles. Fractional reserve banking is one cause of error cycles. Fiat exchange rate stabilization is another cause of these cycles.

they are cautious in making decisions involving, or hinging on, exchange rate movements.

Additionally, investors may think that countries that are highly interconnected in the international financial markets are "too big to fail." This is in fact what some Icelandic bankers themselves thought: other nations would bail them out. The former CEO of Kaupthing Singer and Friedlander, Armann Thorvaldsson, writes,[4]

> I always believed that if Iceland ran into trouble it would be easy to get assistance from friendly nations. This was based not least on the fact that, despite the relative size of the banking system in Iceland, the absolute size was of course very small. For friendly nations to lend a helping hand would not be difficult.

In other words, Thorvaldsson believed that if bad came to worse, other nations would bail Iceland out. However, he had not thought of the interconnectivity of financial markets and the possibility of a worldwide financial collapse. In the fall of 2008, Western countries had their own problems, and they were unable to attend to Iceland's needs.

Investors may have thought it very unlikely, if not impossible, that a highly regarded Western nation would face bankruptcy and the consequent collapse of its currency. Iceland did, after all, consistently score high on the United Nations' Human Development Index; its per capita GDP was among the highest in the world; its workforce was well educated; and its global brand was well known and growing. Each year its already credible list of achievements lengthened. Iceland rapidly extended its financial reach around the world, and rose meteorically to international financial stardom. Many investors did not expect that such a bright star could fall. And even if this rising star should turn into a shooting star, who would *not* rush to Iceland's rescue to prevent a global collapse? The IMF has bailed out economies that were far less integrated with the rest of the world than

---

[4]Thorvaldsson, *Frozen Assets*, p. 194.

Iceland's (Latvia springs to mind). Because of this greater perceived stability, currency mismatching flourished.

There is another reason why the currency mismatch was thought to be unproblematic.[5] Banks thought their offsetting currency swaps would hedge their risks. A currency swap is an exchange of future cash flows denominated in different currencies. It is a product of a post-gold-standard world with a myriad of fluctuating fiat paper monies. Imagine an Icelandic fisherman who sells his fish to the United Kingdom, receiving pounds in payment. He requires krónur to pay his bills, which are incurred in Iceland. At the same time, there may be a British entrepreneur selling Rover cars in Iceland for krónur but paying his mortgage in London with pounds. Both entrepreneurs face currency risk. For instance, the British entrepreneur faces the risk that the króna may depreciate before he is paid for the car. He has to convert his krónur income into pounds to pay the mortgage, but this income may be worth less in the future if the króna depreciates against the pound. The two entrepreneurs may therefore agree on a swap: the British entrepreneur may give some part of his Icelandic króna revenues to the fisherman in exchange for the fisherman's pound revenues at an agreed-upon exchange rate. Because the exchange rate is fixed at inception, they can forget about future exchange rate movements.

It is true that Icelandic banks did buy many swaps to hedge their positions. This gave many people a false sense of security concerning future liquidity constraints. A 2004 IMF report reinforced the belief that the Icelandic banking sector's diversification into foreign markets was a positive development.[6] Although it was true that revenue diversification was not problematic, there was a considerable and growing mismatch between lending in foreign currencies and revenues in the same currencies. In 2004, approximately 20–30 percent of foreign-denominated lending was directed towards firms

---

[5] Juan Ramón Rallo, "¿Qué pasó en Islandia?" *La Illustración Liberal* 41 (2009): p. 46.

[6] IMF, "2004 Staff Visit."

with no offsetting foreign revenues. Instead of questioning the reasons for this growing imbalance or proposing actions to constrain it, the IMF recommended that the financial authorities increase monitoring and regulatory efforts in order to try to resolve potential crises stemming from this mismatch only after they occurred.

In judging that their currency swaps would protect them, the Icelandic bankers did not take into account their concomitant maturity mismatching, which made the swaps insufficient to help them. When short-term foreign debt comes due, there is a sudden need for foreign currency to retire the debt. A currency swap only allows a small sum to be made available each year (or other predetermined time period). For example, imagine that a bank has borrowed €100,000 in order to grant a mortgage of thirteen million Icelandic krónur.[7] It pays €8,000 (eight percent) interest to its creditor and receives 1.3 million krónur from the mortgage holder (ten percent) annually. With a swap, the bank may convert each yearly payment by the mortgage holder (1.3 million krónur) into euros at a fixed rate (let us say 140 krónur per euro). Then the bank has hedged its €8,000 expenses every year by receiving €9,286. However, *the whole mortgage* cannot be converted into euros at any one time. If the bank has borrowed the €100,000 for a short duration and the loan cannot be renewed, then the bank suddenly needs all of the €100,000. It does not help the bank to be able to convert 1.3 million krónur into €9,286, as the bank needs the full amount: €100,000.

As long as foreign central banks continued to offer credit at artificially low interest rates, Icelandic banks had no problems renewing their short-term debts. Their investment-grade rating gave them seemingly unlimited access to foreign wholesale funding. Currency mismatching is, in fact, a way to export credit expansion (or maturity mismatching in general).

---

[7]Our choice of €100,000 is merely illustrative. The Icelandic banking system was entangled in millions of euros of currency swaps, all of which served to create liquidity problems when they could not be renewed.

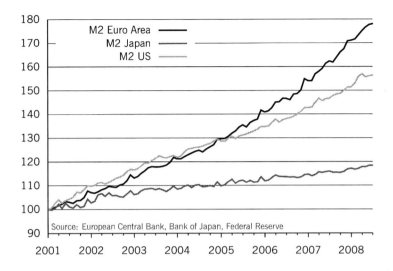

**Figure 5**: Euro area, Japanese yen, and U.S. dollar M2 (January 2001 = 100)[8]

International liquidity had been ample after the September eleventh attacks. Interest rates for borrowing denominated in euros, dollars, and yen were very low. The Federal Reserve held its target interest rate at one percent for nearly a year (from June 25, 2003 to June 20, 2004), the European Central Bank held its interest rate at two percent for two and a half years (from June 6, 2003 to December 6, 2005), and the Bank of Japan held its discount rate below one percent from 2001 to 2008. The monetary inflation pursued by the Fed, the ECB, and the Bank of Japan is shown in Figure 5.

Via currency mismatching, the main economies exported their credit expansion to Iceland. Thus, artificially low interest rates in Europe, the U.S., and Japan deceived entrepreneurs about the availability of real savings not only in their own currency areas but also in Iceland. Not only were Icelanders

---

[8]All figures are monthly. Euro growth is based on end-of-period quantities. Yen quantities are averages over the outstanding period. U.S. dollar figures are not seasonally adjusted.

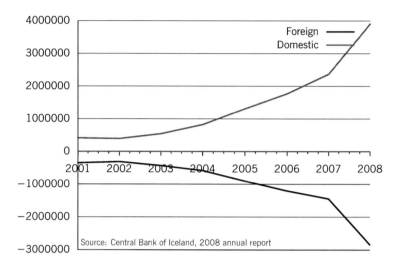

**Figure 6**: Net domestic and foreign assets of the banking system (million króna)

undertaking more investment in foreign currencies than real exchange rate risk would suggest was prudent, but more foreign currency was invested in Iceland than foreigners were saving.

This currency mismatch had reached impressive dimensions. Over the past decade, the Icelandic financial system had accumulated a significant portion of its funding requirements in foreign currencies.

Figure 6 shows the Icelandic banking system's domestic assets minus domestic liabilities on the positive scale, and its foreign assets minus foreign liabilities on the negative scale.

Most shockingly, we draw attention to the increase in foreign liabilities that occurred over the seven-year period: 2,300 percent. Domestic liabilities, in contrast, increased by 600 percent, the result of low nominal interest rates with real rates hovering close to zero.

The Central Bank of Iceland targeted an inflation rate of 2.5 percent (with a band of 1–4 percent) during the 2000s. It regularly overshot this target; *Statistics Iceland* regularly showed

|  | Policy Rate[9] | Targeted Inflation | CPI | Real Interest Rate |
|---|---|---|---|---|
| 2000 | 10.5 | 2.5 | 5.0 | 5.4 |
| 2001 | 10.9 | 2.5 | 6.7 | 4.2 |
| 2002 | 8.4 | 2.5 | 4.8 | 3.6 |
| 2003 | 5.4 | 2.5 | 2.1 | 3.2 |
| 2004 | 6.2 | 2.5 | 3.2 | 2.9 |
| 2005 | 9.4 | 2.5 | 4.0 | 5.3 |
| 2006 | 12.5 | 2.5 | 6.8 | 5.8 |
| 2007 | 13.8 | 2.5 | 5.0 | 8.8 |
| 2008 | 15.6 | 2.5 | 12.4 | 3.2 |

Source: Central Bank of Iceland; Statistics Iceland

**Table 3:** CBI policy rate, inflation and real interest rates (2000–2008)

inflation ranging from four to six percent during the same years (Table 3). The resulting real rates dropped below three percent in 2004, the same year when the CBI was flushing the financial system with credit (over thirty percent of M1 growth) and Iceland's big banks had started aggressively competing in the domestic mortgage market. Banks seized upon these low real rates to expand operations, both in Iceland and overseas.

By 2008 the foreign funding gap (foreign assets minus foreign liabilities) amounted to twenty-two percent of year 2007 GDP. Domestic assets valued at inflated prices apparently filled this gap. In 2008, foreign liabilities amounted to eight times the 2007 GDP.

We can see this divergence in funding sources more clearly if we assess the specific gaps and surpluses on a yearly basis, as is shown in Table 4.

As can be seen, a relatively small foreign funding gap (foreign-denominated assets less foreign-denominated liabilities) in 2001 had grown by 717% over the eight-year run up to the 2008 collapse.

---

[9] Yearly average rate.

|  | Foreign Gap | Domestic Surplus | Foreign Gap Growth (yoy %) | Domestic Surplus Growth (yoy %) |
|---|---|---|---|---|
| 2001 | −348,114 | 412,145 |  |  |
| 2002 | −311,013 | 391,492 | −11 | −5 |
| 2003 | −429,435 | 541,505 | 38 | 38 |
| 2004 | −578,923 | 820,944 | 35 | 52 |
| 2005 | −902,869 | 1,308,025 | 56 | 59 |
| 2006 | −1,202,619 | 1,768,836 | 33 | 35 |
| 2007 | −1,446,475 | 2,368,527 | 20 | 34 |
| 2008 | −2,842,375 | 3,906,646 | 97 | 65 |
|  |  | **Total Growth:** | 717 | 848 |

Source: Central Bank of Iceland, 2008 annual report

Table 4: Domestic and Foreign Funding Gaps (million króna, year-on-year percentage)

It is true that the domestic funding surplus grew at an even wilder pace. Yet, at the end of 2008 as the boom had reached its frenzied extreme, twice as many foreign-denominated liabilities lacked any source of foreign funding as at the beginning of the year. This intense increase in unfunded foreign-denominated liabilities finally culminated as the króna's decline in the foreign exchange markets put a halt to any further foreign acquisitions.

One main source of this external funding was loans denominated in Japanese yen.[10] The Bank of Japan pursued an

---

[10] Approximately eighty percent of foreign-currency loans made to households were denominated in the two currencies with the lowest interest rates, Swiss francs and Japanese yen (Willem H. Buiter and Anne Sibert, "Icelandic Banking Crisis," p. 16). Indeed, Iceland's own domestic policies can hardly have been the lone source of the extreme credit expansion. As the Bank of International Settlements was able to discern after Iceland's collapse, "During the early years of the twenty-first century, the situation on the global financial markets was highly unusual. The supply of credit was virtually inexhaustible and interest rates lower than they had been in a hundred years. Financial markets were hungry for bonds, including those issued by Iceland's

extremely loose monetary policy for many years to combat an extended recession. As a result of these artificially low borrowing rates, yen-denominated loans could be obtained at historically low interest rates, sometimes as low as one percent per annum. Because of these attractive rates, an ample amount of short-term liquidity was available, which in turn was invested in the now famous maturity mismatch. Icelanders invested domestic and foreign short-term funds in long-term investments, leading to inflated assets prices and malinvestments, both at home and abroad. The use of lower interest rate foreign currency financing became a ubiquitous scene in the financial landscape. When given a choice between double-digit interest rates on króna-denominated loans and negligible interest rates on foreign-denominated loans, the latter was almost certainly the preferred choice. As the head of the economics department at the University of Iceland, Gunnar Haraldsson, recounts, "When you bought a car, you'd be asked, 'How do you want the financing? Half in yen and half in euros?' "[11]

Icelandic foreign-denominated credit increased by over 550 percent between 2002 Q4 and 2005 Q4.[12] The low foreign interest rates provided Icelanders with ample liquidity, which they directed into highly profitable investments. Coupled with a strengthening króna exchange rate, this borrowing source was generating profit on its own; borrowed money was repaid in depreciated currency units. The interest rate differential—the now-famous carry trade—was highly profitable for several years. Icelandic banks believed that exchange rate risk was largely hedged, and so they allowed themselves to develop a significant foreign funding gap.[13]

---

banks, which were a welcome addition to many of the structured securities that became so popular" (Ingimundur Friðriksson, "The Banking Crisis in Iceland in 2008," *BIS Review* 22 [2009]).

[11]As quoted in Gumbel, "Iceland: The Country That Became a Hedge Fund."

[12]Honjo and Mitra, "Iceland: Selected Issues," p. 25.

[13]Tchaidze, Annett, and Ong, "Iceland: Selected Issues," p. 26.

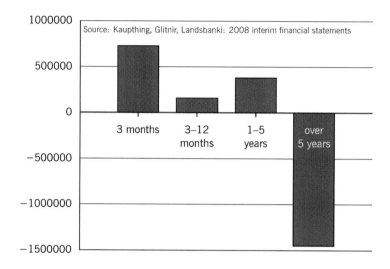

**Figure 7**: Foreign funding gap: big three banks (million krónur)[14]

Icelandic banks issued short-term foreign-denominated liabilities that they would later change into Icelandic krónur at the central bank. Consequently, the Icelandic money supply increased; however, the banks' demand for krónur artificially maintained the króna rate. The newly created krónur were lent to Icelanders on a long-term basis. The result of this combined maturity mismatch and currency mismatch may be seen in Figure 7.

Banks used the leverage of foreign debts to increase their profits. Almost seventy percent of the debts of Icelandic banks were denominated in foreign currency.[15] Some of these debts

---

[14]The foreign funding gap is defined as foreign liabilities minus assets of a certain maturity. A positive funding gap of maturities up to three months means that there are more liabilities coming due in this period than there are assets maturing. The currency breakdown of the term structure of individual banks' assets and liabilities is not publicly disclosed. Therefore, the respective currency mismatches have been calculated assuming the share of foreign-currency assets and liabilities in the balance sheet total is constant over all maturities.

[15]Rallo, "¿Qué pasó en Islandia?"

had been used to make loans in foreign currency. For example, Icelandic banks took on foreign-denominated liabilities to make foreign-denominated loans to Icelandic companies, which used these funds to engage in a spending spree, acquiring companies and assets throughout Europe. Another important part of this foreign debt, 2.5 billion krónur, was used to grant loans denominated in krónur that amounted to almost twice the Icelandic GDP. In other words, the currency mismatch was almost twice the whole island's yearly productive capacity.

Icelandic banks could easily fill this funding gap when the króna was strong relative to these foreign currencies, but as the exchange rate commenced its weakening phase, filling the gap became more difficult. The collapse of the currency created a leak in the financial system that the CBI could not be plug by increasing the money supply. With only depreciating domestic assets to sell to "plug the hole," the banks could not bear the financial drain caused by these foreign loans.

Only approximately 7.5 trillion krónur of foreign-denominated assets were available to finance over ten trillion krónur worth of foreign-denominated liabilities. Even taking into account the available domestic assets, the total asset base of fifteen trillion krónur would just barely be enough to cover the fourteen trillion krónur of debt commitments, both domestic and foreign. Any exchange rate shock would pose a liquidity problem for the banking sector, as liabilities could be met only with some difficulty.

This leveraged financial system heavily funded with foreign liabilities became unsustainable. The reduction in the króna exchange rate created a gap too large to fill through continued sales of domestic assets.

The IMF, to its credit, did note this dangerous development as early as 2004.[16] The Fund expressed concern that most borrowing in the Icelandic financial sector was being undertaken for short durations, and that 20–30 percent of foreign-denominated

---

[16]IMF, "2004 Staff Visit."

loans were made to firms with no offsetting foreign currency revenues. This unhedged position meant that if an adverse exchange rate shock occurred, domestic firms would have little recourse for funding these liabilities except continual reliance on increasingly uncertain króna-denominated sources. This asymmetry exposed many firms to large degrees of exchange rate risk, which became painfully apparent in late 2008 when the exchange rate began collapsing.

In fact, this growing mismatch was recognized, but at the same time its importance was downplayed. In an IMF report on Iceland, Tchaidze, Annett, and Ong[17] wrote that the steady growth in foreign-denominated borrowing "could potentially become an important *indirect* credit risk for banks."[18] In just one year, 2006, foreign-denominated borrowing had increased from sixty-eight percent of GDP to eighty-five percent. This increase was focused in the service, retail, and construction industries, the very industries that had the least amount of foreign revenues to offset the positions and mitigate the risk. It was becoming apparent that this mismatching was predicated on the belief that the CBI would continue pursuing a strong-króna monetary policy, allowing these foreign-denominated loans to be easily repaid.

As long as international liquidity remained high, Icelandic banks faced no problem continually obtaining new short-term funding in foreign currencies. When international short-term liquidity dried up, however, Icelandic banks were left with illiquid long-term assets.

---

[17] Tchaidze, Annett, and Ong, "Iceland: Selected Issues," p. 24.

[18] Tchaidze, Annett, and Ong noted that "banks' foreign-currency lending to households, which has increased sharply, could potentially become an important indirect credit risk as unhedged households may underestimate the impact of currency movements on their debt service costs." (Ibid., p. 32).

# Chapter 5

# The Consequences of the Boom: Malinvestments

Austrian business cycle theory describes the process whereby a general error-induced boom is produced.[1] Credit expansion

---

[1] The Austrian theory of the business cycle was originally developed in Ludwig von Mises (*The Theory of Money and Credit*; *Human Action: A Treatise on Economics* [Auburn, Ala.: Ludwig von Mises Institute, 1949]) and F. A. Hayek (*Prices and Production* [London: Routledge, 1931]; *Profits, Interest, and Investment* [New York: Kelley, 1939]). Additional refinements and additions are found in Richard von Strigl (*Capital and Production*, trans. M. Hoppe and H. Hoppe [Auburn, Ala.: Ludwig von Mises Institute, 1934]), Hülsmann ("Error Cycles"), Roger W. Garrison (*Time and Money: The Macroeconomics of Capital Structure* [London: Routledge, 2001]; "Overconsumption and Forced Saving in the Mises–Hayek Theory of the Business Cycle," *History of Political Economy* 36, no. 2 [2004]: pp. 323–349), Huerta de Soto (*Money, Bank Credit, and Economic Cycles*), Toby Baxendale and Anthony Evans ("Austrian Business Cycle Theory in Light of Rational Expectations: The Role of Heterogeneity, the Monetary Footprint, and Adverse Selection in Monetary Expansion," *Quarterly Journal of Austrian Economics* 11, no. 2 [2008]: pp. 81–93), Philipp Bagus ("Monetary Policy as Bad Medicine: The Volatile Relationship

misdirects spending and investment in three main ways.

First, malinvestments develop from misallocation of capital. Sustainable investments are those investments that are financed out of real savings. An increase in real savings reduces the interest rate, indicating to entrepreneurs that additional resources are available. Entrepreneurs can then engage in more investment projects using the resources that have been saved. Credit expansion implies an increase in the money supply but *not* an increase in real savings. Producing more money, or increasing the supply of credit, does not make more resources available. Credit expansion causes interest rates to fall even though there is no increase in real savings. Interest rates are artificially low. At these reduced rates, investment projects become profitable that would not be profitable with higher rates. Consequently investment projects are undertaken that cannot be successfully completed with the real savings that are available. In the words of Mises,

> The whole entrepreneurial class is, as it were, in the position of a master-builder whose task it is to erect a building out of a limited supply of building materials. If this man overestimates the quantity of the available supply, he drafts a plan for the execution of which the means at his disposal are not sufficient. He oversizes the groundwork and the foundations and only discovers later in the progress of the construction that he lacks the material needed for the completion of the structure. It is obvious that our master-builder's fault was not overinvestment, but an inappropriate employment of the means at his disposal.[2]

Second, consumption increases beyond what it would have been if interest rates had been at their natural higher level. Enticed by the artificially low interest rate, people increase their

---

Between Business Cycles and Asset Prices," *Review of Austrian Economics* 21, no. 4 [2009]: pp. 283–300; "Austrian Business cycle Theory"), and David Howden, ("Knowledge Shifts and the Business Cycle: When Boom Turns to Bust," *Review of Austrian Economics* 23, no. 2 [2010]: pp. 165–182).

[2] Mises, *Human Action*, p. 560.

consumption, thereby reducing their savings. They indebt themselves more and increase their purchases, typically of durable consumers goods.[3]

Third, there is a shift to the sector where credit expansion creates the greatest profits, i.e., the financial sector. An increased money supply filters to the economy via large banks making loans to smaller business and extending consumer credit. By making use of the fresh liquidity prior to its use by others, banks reap profits before Cantillon effects set in. Prices will only rise *after* other firms employ the money. Additionally, as the financial sector endogenously creates new money, extending loans against its deposit base, its profits soar, attracting resources from all over the economy. If this process continues long enough, the banking system fails to maintain its supreme relative profit rates, being surpassed by firms engaging solely in financial speculation. It no longer remains advantageous to earn money solely by relying on the loans to the now dwindling production based economy. Speculation becomes a profit driver, with profits relying on the continual influx of money and credit to maintain price buoyancy.[4] Again, this shift is marked by

---

[3]The increase in consumption goods is most pronounced in the durable goods category. Just as longer-dated production projects are favored as they are relatively more profitable at decreased interest rates than short-term projects, those consumers' goods which are durable will become relatively more valued than nondurables. A longer serviceable life will create greater net present value consumption opportunities as the interest rate is reduced.

[4]Philipp Bagus ("Asset Prices—An Austrian Perspective," *Procesos de Mercado: Revista Europea de Economía Política* 4, no. 2 [2007]: pp. 57–93, "Monetary Policy as Bad Medicine") discusses the herd behavior that results from this process. As the driver of high profits shifts through the economy over time, entrepreneurs chase these disequilibrium opportunities. Since the profits from financial speculation mark the logical conclusion of the necessary link of prices determined by the "vicissitudes of the [underlying] market" (Mises, *Human Action*, p. 810), financial speculation must become rampant, as the continuance of profits relies on a maintained volume of transactions. Entrepreneurs, seeing these maintained or strengthened profits, continue flooding into the financial sector, maintaining or strengthening profits as long as the credit influx remains.

a resource loss not only to the real economy, but also to the previously thriving banking industry.

We will consider in turn how these three distortions of spending and investment developed in the specific case of Iceland.

In the Icelandic case, the malinvestments at home were brought about by the domestic credit expansion, as well as by currency-mismatching investors using foreign-denominated funds to invest in Iceland. Malinvestment also occurred abroad as Icelandic banks borrowed and lent in foreign currencies, allowing Icelandic companies to buy foreign companies and participate in the international credit-induced boom.

The domestic investments financed by maturity mismatching and currency mismatching were mainly in the aluminum smelting and construction industries. Both aluminum smelters and residential and commercial housing are long-term investment projects that were financed by short-term funds, and not by savings of an equal term.

During smelting, aluminum is extracted from its oxide alumina, which in turn is extracted from the ore Bauxite. Iceland has no aluminum mines, but it is endowed with two abundant sources of cheap energy: glacial rivers running from the interior and geothermal heat. While Iceland cannot export energy due to its geographic isolation it can use it for production processes requiring much energy. Aluminum smelters use prodigious amounts of electricity. In this production process, aluminum ore is transported to Iceland, it is smelted using cheap energy, and the aluminum is shipped back to other countries to be used in production processes. At the turn of the century, Iceland already accounted for four percent of worldwide aluminum production.

Aluminum production is a very capital-intensive and time-consuming process, what Eugen von Böhm-Bawerk[5] would have called a very "round about" process. Its viability depends on high savings and low interest rates, as well as high aluminum prices. During the credit boom of 2001–2007 central banks all

---

[5]Eugen von Böhm-Bawerk, *Capital and Interest*, vol. 2, *Positive Theory of Capital* (South Holland, Ill.: Libertarian Press, [1889] 1959).

over the world increased money supplies, resulting in booms in capital-intensive industries. Aluminum, which is a prime input factor for many of these industries, consequently experienced a boom. As aluminum prices soared and interest rates stayed at historic low levels, expanding Icelandic smelting appeared to be profitable. As a result, Iceland became involved in the international asset price bubble.

In 2003 Iceland's parliament, the *Althing*, approved plans to provide new power plants in order to run two additional aluminum smelters. They would be located on opposite sides of the island, east and west. The plant in the west would be geothermal, constructed by the national power company of Iceland, Landsvirkjun, and would be one of the largest hydroelectric power plants in Europe when finished. The total investment would tally to almost $4 billion, about thirty-five percent of Iceland's GDP.[6] Holes would be drilled into the ground and into the volcanic hotbed of the island. Emerging steam would power the generators. In the east, the largest gravel dam in the world would be built, creating a new artificial lake filled with glacier meltwater. Water going through underground tunnels would provide electricity for a new smelter owned by the American aluminum producer Alcoa. The power companies would be public, and would constitute a malinvestment directly financed by the government. The dimensions of these projects were enormous. Operating costs would amount to approximately thirty-five percent of the country's GDP.[7] This was a huge investment that increased foreign debts and the trade deficit, since the investment goods necessary for their construction had to be imported.

The other main domestic malinvestment was made in housing. Houses are a very capital-intensive good with lengthy periods of serviceableness. Decades, or even centuries, may expire before a house is consumed fully. Due to the length of the production and use processes, the construction sector is especially sensitive to interest rates. Low interest rates boost the capital value of houses, making it attractive to build or purchase

---

[6]Thorvaldsson, *Frozen Assets*, p. 150.  [7]Jónsson, *Why Iceland?* p. 64.

them. Interest rates were low not only due to Icelandic credit expansion but also due to currency mismatching, as houses were financed with mortgages denominated in yen or Swiss francs at low rates. The housing boom fueled by currency mismatching is another way that the international credit expansion affected and filtered into the Icelandic economy.

The existence of a particular state institution may explain why a housing bubble developed in Iceland in the first place, or at least why the problem became so exaggerated. The Icelandic government formed the Housing Financing Fund (HFF) in 1999 to provide low-interest mortgages. It is the Icelandic counterpart of America's Freddie Mac and Fannie Mae, with the difference that it deals directly with customers. The U.S. government implicitly guarantees the debt of Freddie Mac and Fannie Mae (which were themselves protagonists in America's housing bubble), but the Icelandic government had gone farther in institutionalizing moral hazard into the HFF's operations; it had explicitly guaranteed the HFF's debt.

In many countries, state-controlled mortgage assistance schemes like the HFF are reserved for those deemed most in need. Icelandic society, however, prides itself on treating everyone equally. (Equality is such an ingrained feature of Icelandic life that passport controls when entering the country do not distinguish between foreigners and Icelanders.) All citizens were given equal access to HFF mortgages provided at artificially lowered rates. The result was increased demand for housing across the board (not just among the lower income brackets, as occurs in other countries). By mid-2004 almost ninety percent of Icelandic households held an HFF loan, and HFF-issued bonds comprised more than half of the Icelandic bond market.

Hunt, Tchaidze, and Westin[8] provided one early warning of the imbalances and dangers that could be created by the HFF. Enhanced access to international capital markets led the big three banks to enter the primary mortgage market for the first time.

---

[8]Hunt, Tchaidze, and Westin, "Iceland: Selected Issues," p. 31.

## The Consequences of the Boom: Malinvestments  57

The HFF had enhanced the efficiency of the mortgage market significantly by the second half of 2004, leading to a sharp increase in mortgage lending and a steep decline in mortgage interest rates. Mortgage lending increased by sixty-three percent during 2004, and most of the increase occurred in the final half of the year. Mortgage rates fell by 5.10 percent in nominal terms, 4.15 percent when adjusted for inflation.[9] Had these efficiency increases been brought on by free competition restrained by the threat of losses, there would have been no immediate cause for concern. Instead, the publicly guaranteed fund was able to reduce mortgage rates unilaterally, enticing unsuspecting homebuyers to take on increasing indebtedness unaware that the situation was unsustainable.

Compared to other countries, the Icelandic government's involvement in the mortgage market was large. Most other Western European countries that encouraged state-guaranteed loans and mortgages did so via a private banking sector. Few countries exhibited widespread public support for a government-controlled mortgage system such as was implemented in Iceland.[10]

At times, the HFF went above its already-lenient core operating mandate. In 2005, the Fund funneled its excess liquidity to the commercial banking system, making approximately eighty billion krónur (around one billion euros) available, an activity not covered in its original mission.[11]

These distortions had long been noted, particularly by the IMF during the HFF's dominance in the mortgage market in the first five years of the 2000s.[12] By August 2006, repeated calls for reform of the HFF had failed, and artificially cheap state-

---

[9] Luckily, the majority of Icelandic mortgages are inflation-indexed, making the inflation-adjusted rates largely moot.

[10] Hunt, Tchaidze and Westin ("Iceland: Selected Issues") provide a comparison of Iceland, Finland, Sweden, Denmark, Germany and France's public mortgage support systems.

[11] Íslandsbanki, ÍSB Weekly (July 26, 2005).

[12] See, for example, International Monetary Fund, "Iceland—2005 Article IV Consultation Concluding Statement" (June 13, 2005) and Tchaidze, Annett and Ong, "Iceland: Selected Issues," p. 32.

guaranteed debt had caused noticeable distortions in the mortgage market.[13] An IMF report from 2005 recommended altering the scope of the HFF's operations:[14] the HFF should assume a role closer to those of the American giants Fannie Mae and Freddie Mac, with operations contained in the secondary mortgage market. Securitizing mortgages and then selling them to investors as mortgage-backed securities, it was reckoned, would provide a more stable mortgage market.

The HFF was a large presence in the mortgage market, but the banks were flush with cash and looking for a way to use it, and they decided to enter the market themselves. They originally offered mortgages at a fixed real interest rate of 4.3 percent. This was lower than the HFF's rate of 4.8 percent. The banks set maturities at twenty-five to forty years. Finally, they removed króna loan limits and allowed a maximum loan-to-value ratio of eighty percent. These features bettered the HFF's offerings on both counts: the state agency had a maximum loan limit of 9.7 million krónur, and its rules allowed for maximum loan-to-value ratios of 65–70 percent.

Mortgages offered through the banks were not limited to construction or housing loans. In contrast to the HFF, the banking system would offer loans towards equity withdrawals or the refinancing of previous mortgages. In an attempt to compete against their state-supported counterpart, Icelandic banks created features previously unknown to Icelandic borrowers. In doing so, they increased the amount of consumer credit beyond anything previously conceivable.

By mid-2004 the HFF had reduced its own rates to remain competitive. All parties were offering mortgages at 4.15 percent. The banks, in an attempt to maintain competiveness both against the HFF and among themselves, increased their lending limits by offering 100-percent mortgages. It was now possible to finance all of your home purchase with borrowed money.

---

[13] Honjo and Mitra, "Iceland: Selected Issues."
[14] Hunt, Tchaidze, and Westin, "Iceland: Selected Issues," p. 42.

The banks soon realized that they were at a disadvantage to the HFF when it came to gross lending power. The Housing Financing Fund could match every change the banks made, whether it be loan-to-value ratios, maximum loan limits, or other related options. Iceland's newly privatized banks, led by the big three, found themselves unable to compete with the state-supported system based on low interest rates alone. Instead, they were increasingly forced to reduce the quality of the collateral posted for their mortgages, an occurrence which resulted in a general underpricing of risk. As price-based competition was all but eliminated due to the equality of interest rates, alternative avenues were sought. Banks were competing aggressively against a state-guaranteed entity that held almost half of the mortgage market.

Typically, banks grant mortgages to only the most creditworthy individuals, those with secure jobs or large amounts of savings, for example. As banks sought additional ways to compete in the mortgage market, they took on less creditworthy individuals as clients. As mortgages could not be sold at higher interest rates lest the borrowers seek lower rates elsewhere, an increasing number of mortgages were issued to people who would previously, and normally, have been considered non-creditworthy individuals. The drive to maintain competitiveness resulted in a general underpricing of risk.[15]

The short-term risk of heavily mismatching the durations of loans and debts was soon overshadowed by the longer-term risk of poorly collateralized mortgages. By 2006, over sixteen percent of new mortgages had loan-to-value ratios greater than ninety percent.[16] By issuing longer-termed mortgages, sometimes up to forty years, in their drive to compete with the HFF, the banks had exposed themselves to greater interest rate risk. By the end of 2006, a two percentage point rise in market interest rates would have caused $465 million in losses

---

[15] Tchaidze, Annett, and Ong, "Iceland: Selected Issues," p. 24.
[16] Honjo and Mitra, "Iceland: Selected Issues."

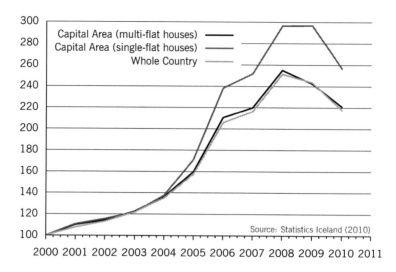

**Figure 8:** Housing prices (2000 = 100)

for the banking sector alone.[17]

Eventually, banks found themselves unable to compete with the HFF in terms of mortgage rates and collateral alone. Risk-adjusted rates of return were suffering from the combined effects of decreased collateral requirements, reduced interest rates, and lower down-payments. Banks began bundling other services, such as insurance, with their mortgages in an attempt to generate ancillary profits from these additional products. Tchaidze, Annett, and Ong[18] noted that "Over the longer-term, such strategies are likely to be unsustainable and could potentially weaken bank soundness."

The interest-rate disadvantage that banks shared relative to the HFF was removed in the summer of 2004 when Kaupthing began to offer the same rates as the HFF.[19] The HFF answered the challenge by lowering its rates and lending at higher loan-to-value ratios. Competitive bidding to get larger shares of the mortgage market ensued, with the banks at a disadvantage to

---

[17] Tchaidze, Annett, and Ong, "Iceland: Selected Issues," pp. 24–5.
[18] Ibid., p. 25.   [19] Thovarldsson, *Frozen Assets*, p. 150.

## The Consequences of the Boom: Malinvestments

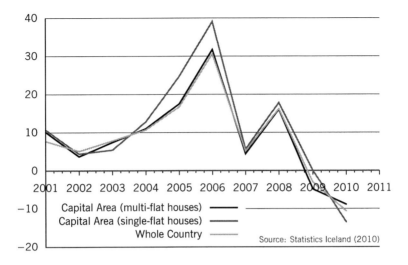

**Figure 9**: Average yearly house price appreciation (percent)

the HFF since they lacked its direct explicit state guarantee.[20]

As mortgage lending skyrocketed, the demand for Icelandic housing did likewise. The immediate result was a steady surge in housing prices, which had already commenced in the late 1990s but really picked up its pace in mid-2004. Every year between 2003 and 2006 saw a greater than ten percent annual price appreciation. In the eight years between 2000 and 2008, housing prices increased by almost 300 percent (see Figures 8 and 9).[21]

---

[20]It is true that the Icelandic banks benefited from CBI guarantee on their liquidity. The main institutional difference is that the banks had private shareholders and were ultimately constrained by the possibility of loan losses. Private shareholders do not favor continual reductions in the interest rate spread as their ensuing profits were commensurately reduced. The HFF, in opposition, was not constrained by this profit motive, and consequently continued lowering mortgage rates irrespective of their profit margin; the HFF did not care so much about profits, being a public entity.

[21]Working for the Central Bank of Iceland, Lúdvík Elíasson and Thórarinn G. Pétursson ("The Residential Housing Market in Iceland: Analysing the Effects of the Recent Mortgage Market Restructuring," Central

The CBI tried to arrest the boom by raising interest rates from 10.5 percent at the end of 2006 to fourteen percent a year later, but this sharp increase did little to restrain the boom. The CBI's action did not strongly affect the rates consumers had to pay to buy houses, which were typically financed with inflation-indexed mortgages, or cars, which were normally financed with foreign loans. Instead, the CBI incentivized the carry trade as the high interest rate attracted foreign investors to invest in krónur. This strengthened the exchange rate, reducing real financing costs for those who were indebted in foreign currency. It also reduced the prices of imports, thus spurring an overconsumption-based boom. This created an unstable situation.

Not only did both the Central Bank of Iceland and the Icelandic government do too little, too late, to arrest the boom that they themselves had caused, but once the bust had begun they took measures that exacerbated it. The HFF made several changes in its lending practices during 2008, just as the boom was collapsing into a severe bust. It increased loan-to-value ratios by more than ten percent and increased maximum mortgage values from eighteen to twenty million krónur.[22] Such changes tended to prevent interest rates from declining to the levels necessary to curtail the boom. Collateral requirements were never seen as problematic, even on the eve of the bust. Jaime Caruana and Ajai Chopra, writing an IMF stability assessment in 2008, noted that nonperforming loans had only increased

---

Bank of Iceland Working Paper no. 29 [2006]) derive a model that shows that structural changes in the Icelandic housing market (i.e., substantial declines in real long-term mortgage rates) led to a strong increase in housing demand. This structural change in the mortgage market led to a permanent lowering of real mortgage interest rates, and contributed to a domestic spending spree and overheating of the economy. The decline in mortgage rates had secondary effects through the economy as funds were freed for other uses.

[22]International Monetary Fund, "Iceland: Article IV Consultation—Staff Report; Staff Supplement; Public Information Notice on the Executive Board discussion; and Statement by the Executive Director for Iceland," IMF Country Report no. 08/367 (2008), p. 15–16.

slightly between 2006 and 2007. Assessing the largest financial institutions, they found ninety percent of them to have loan books of "good quality".[23] As there was no perception of danger from the quality of the collateral on the mortgages they issued, Icelandic banks continued finding investors as well as avenues for investment.

Foreign investors, spurred on by the increasing interest rate differential between Icelandic bonds and still-low foreign ones, started issuing what would later come to be known as the "glacier bond." Denominated in krónur, these bonds gave individuals the ability to invest in the high-yielding country. The first such bond was issued in August 2005 and was internationally heralded because of its high yield relative to low foreign rates coupled with the perception that the Icelandic króna had stabilized and would maintain its high valuation. Issuances reached their apex in the spring of 2007, when $6.3 billion of these bonds were outstanding—equivalent to almost thirty-seven percent of the island's GDP. These glacier bonds were a source of extra liquidity that emerged near the end of Iceland's boom. They came forth at the exact moment when Iceland needed to have its excesses curbed. The liquidity risk that these bonds posed was important, as the carry-trade that the glacier bonds provided led to increasing debt levels for most large financial institutions.[24] As interest rates increased, liquidity flooded in. Icelandic investors poured more money into the many malinvestments, worsening the existing erroneous investments and forming new ones.

Once confidence in the króna became tenuous, additional investments via glacier bonds began to subside. An important short-term source of financing was lost at exactly the moment when the world's supply of short-term liquidity was also waning.

---

[23] Jaime Caruana and Ajai Chopra, "Iceland: Financial System Stability Assessment," p. 16.

[24] Tchaidze, Annett, and Ong, "Iceland: Selected Issues," p. 32.

While we can explain much of Iceland's boom and subsequent bust by the malinvestment of capital along the structure of production, there was also a coincident shift of resources from the production sector into the financial sector. Because the credit injections were made possible via loans issued by the country's banking sector, relative profits increased among these issuers at the expense of the old production-based sectors. The result was a resource shift into the banks, as well as other financial companies.

The extent of these distortions is often unrecognized. As banks expanded their capacity and scope of operations, their own physical resource utilization was increased. Buildings were enlarged, departments were developed, and new employees were hired. What is often missed are the shifts that prepare individuals for a life in banking or finance. Universities altered the courses they offered as demand for certain courses exceeded demand for other, previously more popular, choices.

> "Everyone was learning Black–Scholes" (the option-pricing model), says Ragnar Arnason, a professor of fishing economics at the University of Iceland, who watched students flee the economics of fishing for the economics of money. "The schools of engineering and math were offering courses on financial engineering. We had hundreds and hundreds of people studying finance."[25]

The financial system attracted the talents of the country. Banks offered high salaries to the best students of any discipline even before they finished University. As recently as 2006, starting salaries of £100,000 for new graduates were the norm. "An apocryphal story went that the car park at the university was so full of student cars that the professors had difficulties finding places to park their bicycles."[26]

---

[25] Michael Lewis, "Wall Street on the Tundra: The Implosion of Iceland's Economy," reprinted in *The Great Hangover: 21 Tales of the New Recession*, ed. Graydon Carter, pp. 203–228 (New York: Harper Perennial, [2009] 2010).

[26] Thorvaldsson, *Frozen Assets*, p. 147. Jörg Guido Hülsmann (*The Ethics*

The demand for financiers and bankers displaced the traditional disciplines that had been mainstays of the Icelandic economy and education system. As workers were enticed to work in the increasingly attractive financial industry, the labor force in the real productive sector dwindled. Perhaps more important was the dearth of entrepreneurial talent in the productive sector as the ambitious left for greener financial pastures. Productivity suffered, and the Icelandic economy became more reliant on imported goods. Iceland became an exporter of financial services and an importer of goods. Iceland borrowed foreign money and used it to buy foreign goods, without improving its productivity so as to be able to service this debt in the future; an unsustainable situation was worsening. As Iceland began importing more goods, and at the same time produced fewer "real" goods and services, a substantial trade deficit developed, reaching thirty percent of GDP in 2006, as shown in Figure 10.

This distorted structure of production threatened to starve the population during the currency breakdown in the fall of 2008 when Iceland had problems obtaining foreign exchange to pay for the imports on which the country had become so reliant. Iceland had become dependent on imported goods not only because the economy had lost some of its productive capacity but also because the strong króna made imports relatively attractive. When times were good, Icelanders had access to a nearly endless supply of goods at attractive prices. Attractive, at least, to those fortunate enough to be earning krónur as well as spending them. For foreigners, the strength of the króna made Iceland a financially unattractive travel destination, as even the most mundane items were many multiples more expensive than in even the

---

*of Money Production* [Auburn, Ala.: Ludwig von Mises Institute, 2008], pp. 186–87) explains how an inflationary boom entices individuals to pursue monetary goals in life before those which otherwise would take precedence. Students seeking higher fulfillment through education were soon drawn to the increasingly attractive wages in the financial sector that resulted from inflationary policies, leading them to postpone their studies for immediate monetary goals.

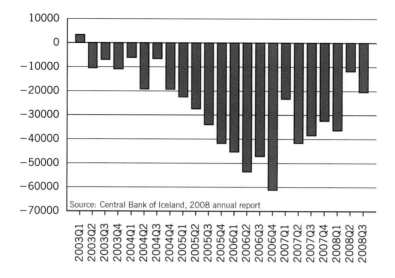

**Figure 10**: Balance of Trade (million krónur)

most expensive European capitals. When the króna weakened, Iceland's dependence on imported goods became a plague. The prices of basic foodstuffs skyrocketed, making previously affluent Icelanders suddenly aware of how tenuous, indeed unsustainable, the previous situation had been.

Icelandic banks and intertwined investment companies made further malinvestments outside the island. They used the ample short-term foreign liquidity to invest in foreign countries, mainly in Great Britain and continental Europe. Because Icelanders were offering generous prices, they found willing sellers of banks, retailers, supermarkets, jewelers, shoe shops, and toy stores. They invested in asset markets by taking on private equity positions, acquiring the British retailers Debenhams, Woolworths, and Hamleys, fully or partly, as well as the Danish companies Magasin du Nord and Royal Unibrew. The FL Group, an international investment company headquartered in Reykjavík, bought a 16.2 percent stake in EasyJet to add to their portfolio that already included Icelandair. The company Baugur, owned by businessman Jon Asgeir, with the help of Kaupthing bought

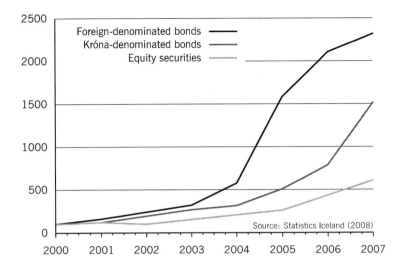

**Figure 11**: Value of securities outstanding (2000 = 100)

the fashion chain Oasis. As Thorvaldsson[27] puts it: "Baugur was also acquiring businesses as if a worldwide ban on takeovers was looming." In November 2006 another Icelandic businessman, Bjogolfur Gudmundsson, bought the English football club West Ham United.

This interest in equity not only drove Icelanders to purchase foreign-listed securities, it also sent the prices of domestic equities shooting upwards. While Icelanders were getting drunk on cheap credit denominated in foreign currencies, they directed only a small portion of the proceeds to similarly denominated assets, as can be seen in Figure 11. Icelandic equities soared in value, increasing over 2,300 percent in value from 2000 to the end of 2007. In 2005 alone, equity values almost doubled.

As long as the international asset-price boom fueled by credit expansion went on, assets kept increasing in price, and so they could serve as collateral for further loans. Icelanders were making big money by using debt to buy foreign companies

---

[27]Thorvaldsson, *Frozen Assets*, p. 134.

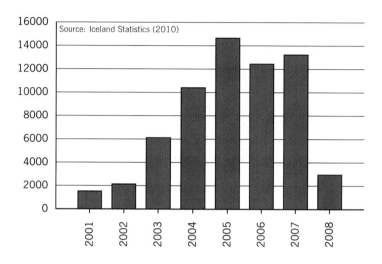

Figure 12: New automobile registrations

during a liquidity-induced asset-price bubble. This brought the Icelanders the nickname of "marauding Vikings," which recalled their ancestors who fell upon Europe destroying and plundering. Likewise, the period between 2000 and 2008 when Icelandic companies were aggressively acquiring foreign companies has been called an "outvasion." In contrast to the Vikings who invaded much of Europe in the middle ages, Icelandic businessmen found that newly created money was better than outright violence for amassing riches.

While the malinvestments increased, eventually shifting into the banking and finally the financing sectors, consumers had commenced consuming beyond their means. Artificially reduced interest rates were not just enticing entrepreneurs to undertake more and longer-dated investments. As the reward for foregoing consumption was artificially reduced, consumers were saving less and consuming the excess. Soaring housing prices, high salaries, and low interest rates made Icelanders feel rich. Since foreign-denominated loans were cheap, Icelanders often used yen-denominated or Swiss-franc-denominated loans to buy cars. As can be seen in Figure 12, new car registrations surged in the mid 2000s. Since Iceland has only about 300,000 citizens, the fact that almost 15,000 new cars were sold in 2005 means that almost five percent of Icelanders bought a new car in 2005.[28]

Iceland often appeared to be a big party. Unemployment rates barely even reached one percent. As businesses were almost fully utilizing the labor force, workers had to be imported. Polish and Lithuanian workers amounted to almost ten percent of the total work force by the end of 2006. The result was that not only were entrepreneurs investing in projects with a first-order effect of insufficient resource availability, but consumers were creating a second-order resource constraint by consuming more. Icelanders soon found themselves working two jobs as business's insatiable hunger for labor could not be satisfied even by temporary migrant workers from Eastern Europe.

Inflation generated overconsumption and new habits. Prudence and conservatism were thrown to the wayside as short-sightedness came into fashion. The inflationary economy increased the time preference of the nation; saving was no longer necessary as easy profits abounded. Nor was it sensible, as inflation quickly removed the purchasing power of any saved money. Consumers rushed to buy flat-screen TVs and cars at artificial low interest rates with a strong króna.

> The older generation shook their heads as their children purchased jacuzzis, trampolines, and chocolate fountains. The sale of champagne increased 82%. The luxury electronics maker Bang and Olufsen sold more in its store in Reykjavik than in any other store worldwide except for Moscow. And amazingly, more Range Rovers were sold in Iceland in 2006 than collectively in the other Nordic countries combined! By the age of fifteen, I had been on a holiday abroad just once…. Now the

---

[28]Proportionately, Iceland's automobile buying boom was about twenty-five percent larger than other developed countries'. Germany, for example, had 3.3 million new registrations in 2005 for a population of eighty-two million: approximately four percent of its population.

typical family was going abroad once or even twice a year. Armani was doing such business in Iceland that they sent a tailor from Italy to make suits to measure.²⁹

The younger population embraced debt, which previous generations had viewed as a thing to avoid. Inflation had made savings a thing of the past; as a corollary, debt was the way of the future. Icelanders had had a taste of the world that debt could provide to them, but had not considered the day of reckoning when the bills would come due. "They had entered a world in which debt—the same debt that had been a ball and chain for their grandfathers—had become a plaything, even sexy. Farmers and fishermen understood derivatives; they took bets on their harvests, their catch".³⁰

Armann Thorvaldsson, former CEO of the Kaupthing subsidiary Singer and Friedlander, tells other stories showing the decadence caused by inflation and the change in habits. Elton John was flown into Iceland to sing on the fiftieth birthday party of one of the country's leading businessmen. New problems confronted the nouveau riche. Service staff, such as drivers or cleaning personnel, had to be trained and instructed. Children were tired of travelling constantly to St. Tropez or Dubai and began crying out to stay at home for vacation. Instead of just drinking gin and tonic, one now had the problem of selecting expensive wines.³¹ Money creation seemed to make wealth creation effortless. Just by cleverly participating in the global liquidity tide while remaining highly and fully leveraged,

---

²⁹Thorvaldsson *Frozen Assets*, p. 156. As Mises similarly described the byproducts of the inflationary process that gripped Germany over eighty years earlier, these effects are "especially strong among the youth. They learn to live in the present and scorn those who try to teach them 'old-fashioned' morality and thrift" (Ludwig von Mises, "Inflation and You," in *Economic Freedom and Intervention: An Anthology of Articles and Essays*, ed. Bettina Bien Greaves, pp. 83–87 [Indianapolis: Liberty Fund, 1942], p. 86). Inflationary periods not only cause the elder generation to feel uneasy about the younger's spending habits, but the younger generation views the restrained elderly with disdain.

³⁰Boyes, *Meltdown Iceland*, pp. 87–88.   ³¹Thorvaldsson *Frozen Assets*, p. 158.

many Icelanders got rich almost without effort. Many of them lost respect for hard work and money. Inflation changed their habits for the worse.[32]

Tony Shearer, who was CEO of the British bank Singer and Friedlander when Kaupthing took it over, was shocked when he started looking into his new employer's books.[33] The giant Icelandic bank had only one board member who was not Icelandic. All directors were hired on four-year contracts, and they were granted loans to buy shares in the bank. The £19 million worth of shares also included embedded options to sell the shares back to the bank at a guaranteed profit.

More troubling, almost all of Kaupthing's stated profits were "earned" by marking up assets it had previously bought at inflated prices. Actual profits related to the activity that used to be known as banking were less than ten percent, as estimated by Shearer.[34]

Hülsmann[35] outlines the financing shift inherent in inflationary conditions. As debtors gain at the expense of creditors, financing becomes increasingly centered on borrowing funds via the banking system or bond markets at the expense of the traditional equity market. The highly inflationary Icelandic environment had shifted the economy into a highly indebted position. Icelandic firms employed debt-to-equity ratios 3.6 times higher than comparable firms in other Scandinavian countries.[36] Another reason why equity funds were a less attractive option than debt-based financing was that the stock market in Reykjavík was small and poorly developed.

Iceland's party was also apparent by a stock market boom. Credit expansion and optimism pushed the Icelandic stock index to ever-greater heights (see Figure 13). With highly leveraged companies, small increases in productivity resulted in huge prof-

---

[32] Hülsmann (*The Ethics of Money Production*, Ch. 13) outlines the effects that a legacy of inflation can have on individuals' personal behavior.

[33] Lewis, "Wall Street on the Tundra." [34] As quoted in Lewis, "Wall Street on the Tundra." [35] Hülsmann, *The Ethics of Money Production*, pp. 179–82.

[36] Hunt, Tchaidze and Westin, "Iceland: Selected Issues," p. 48.

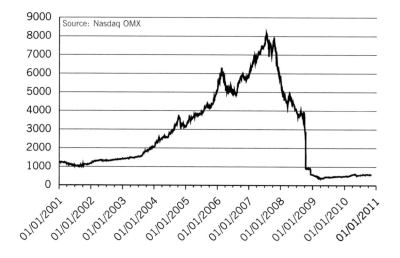

**Figure 13:** Icelandic Stock Market (OMX All Share Index, January 1, 2000–December 1, 2010, krónur)

its. In the three years from 2003 to 2006 the stock market created paper wealth amounting to more than the country's total GDP. The Icelandic stock exchange became home to the second largest prosthetics company in the world (Ossur), the fourth largest pharmaceutical business in the world (Actavis), the UK's largest producer of fresh food (Bakkavor), and France's leading producer of foie gras and smoked salmon (Alfesca).[37] The new wealth provided by higher housing and stock prices spurred overconsumption, overoptimism, and party mood in Iceland.

A significant boom had materialized, much of it realized in foreign currency at captivatingly low interest rates. Borrowing short and lending long, combined with a currency mismatch, had prepared the perfect storm. Iceland had become a kind of hedge fund. Its citizens, companies, and banks had indebted themselves in foreign currency. They had invested for the long term in both foreign- and domestic-denominated assets. With more and more short-term liabilities denominated in foreign currency, a precarious situation loomed.

---

[37] Thorvaldsson, *Frozen Assets*, p. 148.

Chapter 6

# A Timeline of the Collapse

Icelandic banks had no difficulties as long as international liquidity was ample and they could easily renew their short-term foreign-denominated debts. In early 2006, however, problems in the interbank market surfaced, in what would later be called the "Geyser crisis." Price inflation increased and the króna depreciated as foreign money started getting nervous about the sustainability of the Icelandic boom.

Credit default swaps written on Icelandic banks soared. A credit default swap (CDS) is a form of insurance that investors buy to compensate for a loss if a particular debtor defaults on its obligation. Thus, when an investor holds a million-dollar bond issued by Glitnir and the insurance premium is twenty-five basis points or 0.25 percent, he can insure himself against a default by paying an annual fee of 0.25 percent of one million, i.e., $2,500. An intriguing aspect of credit default swaps is that you may buy them even though you do not own any debt issued by the company, Glitnir in this example. Lacking ownership in the underlying company, you are just betting that

Glitnir will default on its obligation. By paying just $2,500 a hedge fund could make a gross profit $1 million if Glitnir defaulted on its obligations. Funds could bet on the downfall of Icelandic banks by buying credit default swaps, and by the very act of buying the swaps they could hope to undermine confidence in the banks and promote their own investment. The CDS spread on a bond is like an insurance premium in that it indicates the confidence in the bond. At the beginning of 2006 investors started to bet against Icelandic banks because of the banks' high dependence on wholesale short-term funding and their burgeoning size, which made them too big to be bailed out by the Icelandic government. As foreign investors increased their demand for protection against defaults by Icelandic banks, the price of the insurance increased in CDS markets; that is, spreads on the banks rose.

At a moment such as this, a vicious spiral may set in. Rising spreads indicate the market's distrust of the banks, spurring even further demand for insurance, leading to even higher spreads on the debt, and so on, until the distrust in the bank reaches a point where the bank cannot receive further funding and it fails. Due to this self-reinforcing spiral of distrust and rising bank funding costs, reputable investors, commentators, and economists (most notably Warren Buffet), have called CDS instruments weapons of mass destruction. Indeed, CDSs can be used to take banks down by lowering the confidence in them. Yet they can only work if banks are vulnerable; that is, if they violate the golden rule of banking and mismatch maturities, or they mismatch currencies, or they do both. Only then will the distrust translate into funding problems that threaten the bank's liquidity and eventually its solvency. When the bank matches maturities and currencies and holds 100 percent reserves to cover its deposits, the distrust may lead to a loss of consumers as some depositors do not continue rolling their funding over; that is, they withdraw their deposits. This, however, will not take down the bank, as no liquidity loss will result. Only a mismatch makes the banks vulnerable to this type of failure.

In the Geyser crisis, international hedge funds attacked Iceland's leveraged and mismatched banking system, as well as its government, by shorting the currency and the bonds of the banks via credit default swaps. Even the government's own bonds were not immune to this attack. Iceland became an international headline. Banks tried to defend themselves against the distrust by pointing to their stellar ratings from the rating agencies. Yet high default swap spreads indicated a general distrust of the Icelandic financial system. Newspaper articles about the faltering currency and the widening CDS spreads further eroded confidence in the banks, causing the spreads to widen. The króna weakened, making the situation a focal point of media attention. The market view that the Icelandic banks would not be able to refinance themselves turned into a self-fulfilling prophecy, but only because the financial system was vulnerable due to its mismatching and credit expansion. Credit default swaps would eventually reach almost 1,000 basis points; the cost to insure $1,000 of debt was almost $100.

Yet Iceland's time had not yet run out. As Armann Thorvalddsson, himself a leading Icelandic banker, recognizes, "What eventually got us out of the situation was the fact that the world was still drowning in liquidity. Although the European bond market had had its fill of Icelandic bank exposure, money was available from other markets at a price."[1] Market participants realized that Icelandic banks still had access to funding and would not yet become illiquid. Moreover, the CBI increased interest rates (from 9 to 12.75 percent) to attract foreign funds and raise confidence. The króna stabilized and CDS spreads narrowed gradually, though they never reached their previous low levels. The collapse was prevented for the time being. Thanks to the ample liquidity in the interbank markets, the party could continue. From 2006 to 2007, asset prices soared, for everything from companies to wine to fine art. Everyone in Iceland seemed to become a millionaire. Even so, Icelandic

---

[1]Thorvaldsson, *Frozen Assets*, pp. 172–73.

**Figure 14**: Króna exchange rates[2]

banks became somewhat more cautious and tried to improve their liquidity situation. Landsbanki tried to increase its access to wholesale funding markets by tapping the internet deposit market with Icesave, an online retail bank that attracted billions of pounds when it opened in the UK. Kaupthing followed suit with its own internet deposit platform, Kaupthing Edge.

In August 2007, when BNP Paribas suspended three investment funds that had invested heavily in subprime mortgages, liquidity in the interbank markets was again constrained, despite several central bank interventions. Icelandic banks soon encountered renewed problems in refinancing their short-term debt. They had no other option than to borrow krónur from the CBI to exchange for foreign currency. As a consequence, the króna started to depreciate, not only against the world's major fiat currencies but against the timeless hard money par excellence, gold. The price of gold doubled in krónur during 2008.

In March 2008, with the tensions connected with the bailout of the investment bank Bear Stearns, the króna lost even more value.

---

[2]Prices are per unit of currency. Gold prices are krónur per 1/1000 ounce.

Icelandic banks, such as Kaupthing, tried to shrink their balance sheets to reduce króna exposure. UK newspapers started writing about the problems of the Icelandic banks, drawing attention to the fact that British depositors were already withdrawing their funds and causing still others to start doing so. The Icelandic government and the Icelandic banks responded with a public relations campaign to restore confidence. The government and the central bank also worked on a bond sale to boost currency reserves. In May, the króna was collapsing but an emergency loan from the Swedish, Norwegian, and Danish central banks of €1.5 billion aided the CBI by almost doubling its foreign reserves. The CBI tried to defend its currency by raising interest rates to fifteen percent in September 2008 in order to entice foreign investors to convert their currencies into krónur and invest more heavily in the island. The falling króna caused problems for bank clients in Iceland who had debts denominated in foreign currency. The quality of loans to these clients deteriorated substantially. As Thorvaldsson[3] describes the situation, "One of the large mistakes made by Kaupthing during the crisis was not to cut down the stock market positions of its best clients more aggressively. When they began to deteriorate the bank continued to support them." But at this point there was almost no alternative. If one of the bank's best clients went bankrupt, they would take the bank down with them.

In September 2008, events followed in quick succession. Banks suffered high losses due to malinvestments, mainly in the housing sector. Even though Icelandic banks had low exposure to the U.S. subprime market, the crisis in that market took its toll. In many countries, the loss of confidence and the fear of further credit losses and insolvencies triggered a run on the banking system. Wholesale investors—banks, large companies, pension funds, insurance companies, and investment funds (hedge funds, short-term fixed-income funds, and money market mutual funds)—withdrew their money from banks. Short-term funding dried up and banks were unable to roll their loans over.

---

[3] Thorvaldsson, *Frozen Assets*, p. 196.

The event that contributed most to this accelerating loss of confidence was when the investment bank Lehman Brothers filed for U.S. Chapter 11 bankruptcy protection. This watershed event occurred on September 15, 2008. The world financial system would never be what it had been before.

Lehman Brothers was broadly exposed to residential mortgages as well as commercial property funded by short-term borrowing.[4] During the late summer of 2008 Lehman's share price eroded and confidence declined. Lehman's losses threatened to wipe out its shareholders' equity. Over the weekend of the thirteenth and fourteenth of September, U.S. authorities tried to save Lehman Brothers by organizing a takeover deal similar to the one that had "rescued" Bear Stearns by having JP Morgan purchase its assets with the backing of a Federal Reserve–brokered loan. As investors of the proposed rescue plan wanted the U.S. Treasury to guarantee them against substantial losses, no deal was achieved on time, and when markets opened on the morning of Monday the fifteenth, Lehman made its bankruptcy filing.

This event caused a panic in the global money markets. If Lehman had been able to hide enormous losses for such a long time, what were other banks hiding? And who, exactly, would be affected by the bankruptcy of Lehman Brothers? Due to the interconnectivity of the banking system, the loss of Lehman would cause losses for other banks, and they might be forced into bankruptcy as well. Most importantly, why was Lehman allowed to fail? Why was Bear Stearns rescued and Lehman not? This raised doubts about the implicit guarantee of a bailout. If the authorities had not considered Lehman to be too big to fail then other banks were in grave danger too. Conversely, if Lehman had been considered too big to bail then how many other precariously positioned banks were also too large to be saved?

---

[4]Alistar Milne, *The Fall of the House of Credit. What Went Wrong in Banking and What Can Be Done to Repair the Damage?* (Cambridge, UK: Cambridge University Press, 2009), p. 286.

On the same day, the debt of American Insurance Group (AIG) was downgraded, triggering a dramatic withdrawal from money market mutual funds. As a result, one money market mutual fund, Reserve Primary, had to freeze withdrawals to save liquidity. Several other funds "broke the buck": the value of the fund's assets fell below the value of the money invested in them. These funds could no longer honor withdrawals at par. Money market mutual funds, which are one of the safest investments, and one considered by many to be a cash equivalent, suddenly seemed not so safe.

Confidence eroded as pressures mounted on all banks that depended on short-term wholesale funding. In the United Kingdom, the Bank of England rescued the Halifax Bank of Scotland. Stability was short lived, however. Once the regulatory authorities supported one bank, the next weak bank in line presented a new danger of destabilization. The Royal Bank of Scotland was the next British bank to find itself in stormy waters as funding became less available. The British government could only stabilize the bank on October 8, when it announced an emergency funding package aimed at supporting all British banks.

As liquidity evaporated, many investors and banks had to sell their assets at fire sale prices to redeem their liabilities. Asset prices consequently collapsed, placing further pressure on bank capital and weakening investors' confidence.

Doubts arose concerning the soundness of the American investment banks Morgan Stanley and Goldman Sachs, which had secured capital from outsiders. These two banks could be stabilized for a short while, but the Federal Deposit Insurance Company (FDIC) shut down another American giant, Washington Mutual, on Thursday the twenty-fifth of September. The British bank Bradford and Bingley was nationalized on September 29 and the U.S. bank Wachovia was taken over, first by Citigroup and later by Wells Fargo when the latter offered a better bid.

In continental Europe, too, the business model of maturity mismatching—borrowing short and lending long—proved to be a lethal combination when confidence eroded and short-term credit evaporated.

On Monday the twenty-ninth of September the bank Fortis was supported by the Benelux countries (Belgium, the Netherlands, and Luxemburg). The German bank Hypo Real Estate, which was dependent on short-term wholesale funding, was saved the same day via a €35 billion loan guaranteed by the German government. Shortly thereafter, Benelux was called upon again to provide capital injections, this time to Dexia, the Belgian-French financial group.

The liquidity squeeze also affected Icelandic banks, which were reliant on wholesale funding. Retail deposits backed only thirty percent of their balance sheets. Retail funding tended to be less fugitive during the crisis than short-term wholesale funding. This stability arose from the deposit guarantees that retail depositors enjoyed, and which their wholesale counterparts lacked.[5] In fact, the Icelandic internet-based bank Kaupthing Edge received an increasing stream of deposits, guaranteed and insured in amounts up to £35,000 by the British government.[6]

The problem for the Icelandic banks was that they had not financed their long-term assets with long-term liabilities but with short-term loans that needed to be continually rolled over. In September 2008 the interbank loan market where they secured this short-term funding dried up. If they had financed themselves with krónur, the CBI could have saved Icelandic banks with króna loans. However, they had financed themselves largely in foreign currency. The combined currency and maturity mismatch meant their end.

Icelandic banks had no alternative other than to sell their long-term assets, foreign and domestic. Due to the currency mismatch, they had to exchange the revenues from the sale of

---

[5] Milne, *The Fall of the House of Credit*, p. 295.

[6] In a similar movement massive flows of money left the UK banking system when Ireland guaranteed all their deposits, even though each depositor openly knew it was an economy in a worse position than the UK, and with a poorer banking system; moral hazard writ large.

their domestic assets for krónur to pay the short-term foreign debt. As the króna exchange rate plunged they had to sell ever more króna-denominated assets to get the foreign currency they needed. Soon they were selling their domestic and foreign assets at near fire sale prices.

As funding dried up in early 2008, all three big Icelandic banks attempted to wind down their positions, both in magnitude and in the extent to which they were mismatched. Glitnir was by far the bank in the worst shape as 2008 progressed, or at least its liquidity issues were the most pressing. With more than 360 billion krónur more in foreign-denominated liabilities coming due within the next three months than it had assets to cover them, Glitnir was only one maturity term away from a serious liquidity crunch. During the first half of 2008 the bank worked furiously to reduce its exposure, and managed to cut down its unmatched short-term foreign positions by more than fifty percent.

Landsbanki was not faring much better. Despite all efforts to reduce its foreign exposure, by June 2008 the bank still needed over 140 billion krónur in foreign funds within the next three months to remain solvent. The bank had plenty of assets, both in krónur and foreign currencies, but they were locked away at the long end of the maturity spectrum. If the bank could remain solvent for *only* another five years, more than 100 billion krónur of foreign funding could be made available when the assets it had splurged on during the boom matured. But the bank would be lucky to get by for another five weeks, let alone five years.

Kaupthing suffered its own problems through its UK subsidiary, Kaupthing Edge, an online deposit bank aimed at attracting foreign depositors with its high interest rates. As the year 2008 progressed, the bank was flush with cash. More than 400 billion krónur sat in its coffers awaiting a good use. As the year wore on and depositors grew increasingly doubtful of the bank's solvency, redemptions intensified. Internet bankers may be more fickle than the average depositor. Kaupthing's British clients had no reason for doing business with Kaupthing

|  | Domestic Funding Gap | | | Foreign Funding Gap | | | Total Funding | | |
| --- | --- | --- | --- | --- | --- | --- | --- | --- | --- |
|  | December 31st, 2007 | June 31st, 2008 | Percent change | December 31st, 2007 | June 31st, 2008 | Percent change | December 31st, 2007 | June 31st, 2008 | Percent change |
| **Kaupthing** | | | | | | | | | |
| On demand | −13,929 | 30,926 | −322 | −406,202 | −221,035 | −46 | −420,131 | −190,109 | −55 |
| < 3 months | 108,392 | 111,307 | 3 | 252,558 | 321,626 | 27 | 360,950 | 432,933 | 20 |
| 3–12 months | 28,980 | 39,797 | 37 | 3,775 | −71,097 | −1,983 | 32,755 | −31,300 | −196 |
| 1–5 years | 101,845 | 101,776 | 0 | 184,887 | 69,007 | −63 | 286,732 | 170,783 | −40 |
| > 5 years | −38,123 | −52,294 | 37 | −578,614 | −767,719 | 33 | −616,737 | −820,013 | 33 |
| **Landsbanki** | | | | | | | | | |
| On demand | not reported | not reported | — | not reported | not reported | — | not reported | not reported | — |
| < 3 months | 100,580 | 80,981 | −19 | 222,473 | 143,583 | −35 | 323,053 | 224,564 | −30 |
| 3–12 months | −13,847 | 31,535 | −328 | −61,792 | 62,549 | −201 | −75,639 | 94,084 | −224 |
| 1–5 years | −39,696 | −10,677 | −73 | −175,844 | −99,815 | −43 | −215,540 | −110,492 | −49 |
| > 5 years | −59,676 | −21,421 | −64 | −221,421 | −105,558 | −52 | −281,097 | −126,979 | −55 |
| **Glitnir** | | | | | | | | | |
| On demand | 81,925 | −40,871 | −150 | 359,072 | 152,887 | −57 | 440,997 | 112,016 | −75 |
| < 3 months | 25,147 | −4,616 | −118 | 103,005 | 48,977 | −52 | 128,151 | 44,361 | −65 |
| 3–12 months | −31,551 | 6,483 | −121 | 7,905 | 143,538 | 1,716 | −23,646 | 150,021 | −734 |
| 1–5 years | 34,427 | 53,568 | 56 | 285,671 | 373,317 | 31 | 320,098 | 426,885 | 33 |
| > 5 years | −362,263 | −339,077 | −6 | −673,308 | −594,641 | −12 | −1,035,571 | −933,718 | −10 |

Source: Kaupthing, Glitnir, and Landsbanki 2008 interim financial statements

**Table 5**: The big three banks' funding gaps (million ISK)[7]

other than its attractive interest offerings. As the bank's security came into doubt, its internet clients vanished as quickly as they had appeared, taking a substantial portion of the bank's deposits with them. During the first half of 2008 Kaupthing hemorrhaged forty-six percent of its foreign assets.[8]

All three large banks were furiously selling assets to cover their burgeoning liabilities. This had its own consequences as the banks were collateralized primarily by equity holdings whose values did not hold up well when not just one but all three of the small country's largest financial institutions were holding a giant fire sale.

Due to this fire sale, the Icelandic stock market plunged as bank valuations based on plunging asset values deteriorated. All over the world, maturity-mismatched investors were finding themselves in similar positions. As a liquidity squeeze emerged, global investors sold assets and rushed to hard currency. As a result, asset prices collapsed. Icelandic banks suffered severe losses on their asset holdings. A double-edged sword cut them: the fire sale of long-term assets in the panic and the reduction of depreciating króna proceeds into foreign funds. Haircuts for Icelandic banks kept increasing. For the same amount of posted collateral they received a diminishing amount of funding.

On September 29, the Icelandic government announced it would take a seventy-five percent equity stake in Glitnir, the weakest of the big three Icelandic banks, for 600 million krónur. In contrast to Landsbanki and Kaupthing, Glitnir was entirely reliant on wholesale funding. Owing to the government insurance scheme, it had failed to attract a demand deposit base that was more stable than the short-term debt financing it would

---

[7]Calculated as liabilities less assets, as at December 31, 2007, and June 30, 2008. The currency breakdown of the term structure of individual banks' assets and liabilities is not publicly disclosed. Therefore, the respective currency mismatches are calculated assuming the share of foreign-currency assets and liabilities in the balance sheet total is constant over all maturities.

[8]This was especially damaging as the Icelandic banks typically relied on retail deposits as a more stable source of funding than the capital markets

continually need to roll over to remain liquid. The bank faced a looming $750 million worth of debt repayment, coming due on October 15. It lacked the funds, and there was little hope of finding a lender, given the prevailing credit situation. The government never carried out its plan to take an equity stake in Glitnir. Before shareholders could approve the plan, the Icelandic Financial Supervisory Authority put Glitnir into receivership.

This intervention triggered a loss of confidence in the Icelandic banking model and a run on the other two big banks. Over the weekend of October fourth and fifth, British newspapers wrote on the extensive leverage of Icelandic banks and the nationalization of Glitnir. In an article titled "Markets call time on Iceland," BBC business editor Robert Preston wrote,

> The best way of seeing Iceland is as a country that turned itself into a giant hedge fund.... Here are the lethal statistics about Iceland: the value of its economic output, its GDP, is about $20bn; but its big banks have borrowed some $120bn in foreign currencies.... Or to put it another way, Iceland simply doesn't have the domestic earnings to service this kind of debt.[9]

An article in *The Guardian* complemented this grim outlook. Tracey McVeigh proclaimed, "The party's over for Iceland," later adding,

> Iceland is on the brink of collapse. Inflation and interest rates are raging upwards. The króna, Iceland's currency, is in free-fall and is rated just above those of Zimbabwe and Turkmenistan. One of the country's three independent banks has been nationalised, another is asking customers for money, and the discredited government and officials from the central bank have been huddled behind closed doors for three days with still no sign of a plan.

---

(see, for example, Landsbanki's 2008 annual report).
    [9]Robert Preston, "Markets Call Time on Iceland," *BBC News* (October 4, 2008).

International banks won't send any more money and supplies of foreign currency are running out.[10]

The news coverage caused a run on Icesave, the online retail bank of Landsbanki in Great Britain and the Netherlands. When Icesave's internet site went down due to volume, depositors further spurred on the run as they worried that the bank had collapsed. The British run on the bank's deposits was especially damaging since sixty-five percent of Landsbanki's short-term deposits were denominated in pounds.[11]

On Monday October 6, Icelandic Prime Minister Geir H. Haarde addressed the nation in a dramatic speech on national television announcing that "There is a very real danger, fellow citizens, that the Icelandic economy, in the worst case, could be sucked with the banks into the whirlpool and the result could be national bankruptcy." His ending the speech with "God save Iceland" contributed to the general atmosphere of doom.[12]

The panic soon reached the public, with Icelanders queuing at banks to withdraw cash. Violence erupted in the normally serene country as Polish workers were not allowed to change their salaries into Euros at some banks. The interbank markets completely shut out the Icelandic banks on October 6. To prevent further bank runs in Iceland, the government fully guaranteed *domestic* retail deposits.

On Tuesday October 7, the Icelandic Financial Supervisory Authority placed Landsbanki into receivership. The British government used the Banking Special Provision Act to transfer deposits from Landsbanki's UK subsidiary Heritable Bank to a

---

[10] Tracy McVeigh, "The Party's Over for Iceland, the Island That Tried to Buy the World," *The Guardian* (October 5, 2008).

[11] Li Lian Ong and Martin Čihák, "Of Runes and Sagas: Perspectives on Liquidity Stress Testing Using an Icelandic Example," IMF working paper WP/10/156 (2010), p. 13. Landsbanki would eventually lose almost half of its pound funding, as forty-three percent of British account holders withdrew their deposits during the bust (Ibid., p. 17).

[12] Geir H. Haarde, "Address to the Nation, Prime Minister's Office," (October 6, 2008).

Treasury holding company. Glitnir was put into receivership the same day.

The events of that day culminated with a memorable telephone conversation between the UK Chancellor of the Exchequer Alistair Darling and the Icelandic Finance Minister Árni Mathiesen. Darling tried to find out if the Icelandic government would guarantee UK deposits of Icelandic subsidiaries. While the Central Bank had guaranteed all domestic deposits, they had not guaranteed foreign ones. Mathiesen would not give such a guarantee, and later that evening Davíð Oddsson, chairman of the board of governors of the Central Bank of Iceland, announced in a broadcast interview that the government would not pay the debts of heedless banks.

As a reaction, and in order to defend the interest of British depositors, Darling announced that the British authorities would freeze Landsbanki's UK assets at the opening of business the next morning. The freezing order used a provision from the Anti-terrorism, Crime, and Security Act of 2001. The sale of Landsbanki's assets within the United Kingdom was effectively prohibited. The UK government compensated British retail deposit holders for an estimated four billion pounds. Gordon Brown even announced that the UK would sue Iceland if it did not compensate the 300,000 affected British savers, and additional Icelandic assets in the UK would be frozen. Icelanders were outraged that a provision of anti-terrorism legislation would be used against them, a country that had for decades allowed the British and American navies to establish bases on its shores to fight their own battles. In fact, for many Icelanders, the announcement that the anti-terrorism legislation would be used against them "was tantamount to a declaration of war. At one stroke Britain had placed Iceland on the same level as Al Quaeda, even though it was a fellow NATO partner, and crippled what seemed to Reykjavik to be a healthy bank."[13]

---

[13] Boyes, *Meltdown Iceland*, p. 174.

Meanwhile the conflict between the United Kingdom and little Iceland provoked even more distrust of the Icelandic banks. By declaring Icelandic bankers to be the legal equivalent of terrorists, the British government had all but sealed the fate of the Icelandic banking industry's foreign branches. Retail investors fled the Icelandic banks. There was a run on Kaupthing Edge, the internet banking arm of Kaupthing's UK subsidiary Kaupthing Singer and Friedlander. The UK Financial Services Authority (FSA) took Kaupthing Singer and Friedlander into administration the same day. Kaupthing's Swedish subsidiary, Kaupthing Bank Sverige was rescued by a credit facility of five billion Swedish krona (€530 million) the same day.

Kaupthing was placed in receivership on October 9. After its UK subsidiary had been placed in administration, the bank was cut off from all credit markets and had to default on its loan agreements. Its subsidiaries in Luxembourg, Geneva, Helsinki, and the Isle of Man quickly defaulted also. Effectively, the financial markets wiped out all three major banks in a matter of days. In contrast to the other cases we have mentioned of banks that ran into trouble during the world financial crisis, such as German, British, or U.S. banks, the Icelandic banks were simply too big to save with the country's modest resources. Even the central bank could not save them, due to their enormous obligations denominated in foreign currency.

This had a major effect on what was left of Iceland's financial system. The Central Bank of Iceland demanded new collateral for their outstanding loans to the remaining financial institutions, because the old collateral consisting of shares in Glitnir, Landsbanki and Kaupthing had become almost worthless. This took down *Sparisjóðabanki*, a bank jointly owned by the country's twenty-one savings banks to provide wholesale and investment services, when it could not provide new collateral. *Sparisjóðabanki* sought government aid to avoid insolvency and the contagion problem this would have caused for related domestic savings institutions.

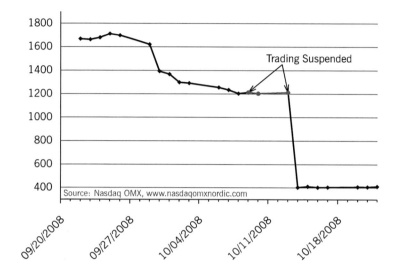

**Figure 15:** OMX Iceland All-Share Index (daily close, September 22–October 22, 2008, krónur)

Only three years earlier the IMF, through its Deputy Managing Director, Anne Krueger, had implicitly promised support in case of a crisis. Entrepreneurs developed investment plans under the assumption that such IMF assistance would be available. The artificially strong króna sustained by implicit support guarantees from the IMF had allowed the economy to soar to breathtaking heights and then come crashing down to earth, and now the IMF was leaving Iceland to fend for itself.

The country was on the verge of total financial collapse. For three days, from the ninth to the thirteenth of October, stock market trading in Iceland was suspended. When the market reopened on Tuesday October 14, it lost sixty-seven percent in a single day. The credit crunch had wiped out many companies listed on the stock exchange, including the largest clients of the banks, further damaging bank loan portfolios.

The sudden decline in the stock market would reverberate through the Icelandic economy more quickly and detrimentally than in other countries. Icelandic banks were not exposed to the subprime loan market, but they were heavily securitized.[14] As security prices were halved by the hour, capital and collateral values evaporated.[15]

Housing prices began to crash. Overextended mortgage holders who had denominated their loans in foreign currencies during the boom now found themselves unable to maintain payments during the bust. As the króna exchange rate deteriorated, their mortgages denominated in Japanese yen and Swiss francs became ever more burdensome to hold. The swift deterioration of the króna exchange rate, particularly during the last half of 2008, left debtors with no time to negotiate more prudent and sustainable loans. The Swiss franc gained 107 percent in value against the króna during 2008. The yen gained 145 percent. Icelandic mortgage holders who had benefited from the low interest rates these currencies offered during the boom now saw their monthly payments increase by 100 to 150 percent in a few months. Less than a decade earlier, economists heralded the inception of the floating exchange rate as a harbinger of future stability.[16] Now Iceland's stability was crumbling, thanks in part to the floating rates.

Iceland's financial markets lay in tatters. The total debt of Icelandic banks was eleven times the country's GDP, and a large part of it was denominated in foreign currencies. In October 2008 the foreign debts of the island were thirty-two times higher than the foreign exchange reserves of the Central Bank of Iceland. Because of the financial collapse, the liabilities

---

[14] Thorvaldsson *Frozen Assets*, pp. 178–79.

[15] Iceland's equivalent to the United State's Dow Jones Industrial Average, the "OMX Iceland 15," listed the fifteen companies with the highest market capitalization listed on the OMX Iceland Stock Exchange. At the point of the crash's apex on October fourteenth 2008 the big three Icelandic banks comprised seventy-three percent of the index's value and witnessed their value completely erased. The index was discontinued in July 2009 and replaced with a new benchmark index, the "OMX Iceland 6." Notably, three of the six companies listed on this new benchmark index comprising approximately one third of its total value (as at November 1st, 2010) are Faroese.

[16] Eduardo Aninat, "IMF Welcomes Flotation."

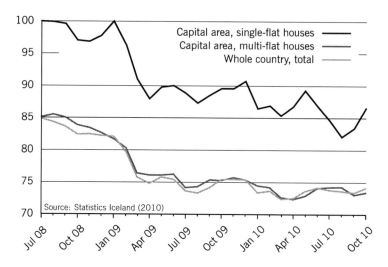

Figure 16: Housing prices (July 2008 to October 2010, capital area single flat houses = 100)

of the Central Bank of Iceland—the monetary base of the króna—were backed mostly by loans to an insolvent banking system. Collateralized by worthless assets and by loans to a government that had taken over crushing foreign liabilities, the CBI could not stem the tide without outside help.

When the Icelandic financial system had come under pressure in the last days of September 2008, the decline of the króna had accelerated. No one wanted the currency of a bankrupt financial system, and Icelandic banks were converting their króna-denominated assets into the foreign currencies they needed to pay foreign-denominated debts. In one of the shortest-lived currency pegs in history, the Central Bank of Iceland tried to peg the króna to the euro at a rate of 131 krónur. Fixing a rate far above what the market could bear resulted in a tremendous excess demand for euros. Investors fled from the króna to the euro. Only two days later, on October 8, 2008, the peg was abandoned, and by October 9, the króna had already collapsed to 340 to the euro as the government took over Kaupthing. With the króna in free fall, the central bank of Iceland reverted to its last resort of intervening in the foreign exchange market. It restricted the purchase of foreign currency within Iceland. From the ninth of October to the third of December here was no free currency market in Iceland.

By October 2008, the outflow of foreign exchange had become so severe that further action was necessary. The CBI issued a memorandum to its member banks outlining measures to facilitate the retention of any foreign reserves they held or were receiving.[17] Banks could only give foreign exchange for expenditure abroad to those clients in possession of a travel ticket or other proof of exiting the country. Bankers would exercise discretion with their clients, focusing on providing foreign currency only for the necessary importation of essential goods; the CBI recommended that foodstuffs, pharmaceuticals, oil products, and public expenditure abroad be considered priority categories. Banks were to avoid using foreign currency for financial-related activities. Banks with access to the central bank's credit facilities would have to submit special accounting records, itemizing their foreign currency transactions daily.

By January 2009, the central bank was exchanging only a negligible amount of foreign currency for domestic krónur. During December 2008, for example, a net sale of €11.1 million was made, of which some €10.8 million was derived from Treasury notes owned by nonresidents, which could be exchanged for foreign currency.

With the currency markets officially closed, the only way to obtain foreign currency was through central bank auctions. The Central Bank of Iceland was auctioning off its foreign exchange reserves, losing $289 million during October 2008.

On November 28, new regulations were imposed to control foreign exchange. Investors, both domestic and foreign, could only move capital in and out of Iceland with a license from the central bank. Thus, foreign investors would be required to

---

[17]Central Bank of Iceland, "New Rules on Foreign Exchange Balance," Press release no. 18/2008 (June 4, 2008), "Temporary Modifications in Currency Outflow," (October 10, 2008).

obtain a license prior to selling their króna-denominated assets. Icelanders were required to deposit all foreign currency they received with an Icelandic bank. In response, several Icelandic exporters fled the increased control and scrutiny to informal offshore markets where they could conduct foreign exchange transactions away from the watchful eye of a regulator.

Foreign aid was necessary to arrest the free fall of the króna. Swap lines from sympathetic countries made foreign exchange available to pay for imports that the Icelandic economy needed but was unable to produce. Iceland's economy had become so distorted, focusing heavily on the financial industry, that it was unable to produce sufficient goods and services to provide capital for the needed imports. Foreign exchange reserves and foreign loans paid for necessary imports. These foreign loans gave the central bank reserves to back up the króna, and gave the Icelandic economy time to restructure.

In the first days of October 2008, a team of experts from the International Monetary Fund came to talk to the government about aid to stabilize the króna. On October 7, the day that the Icelandic government announced that the talks were favorable and that resolution neared, the same day that it placed Landsbanki into receivership, one of the most bizarre events of the Icelandic tragedy occurred. The Central Bank of Iceland announced that it had negotiated with the Russian ambassador, Victor I. Tatarintsev, for a possible €4 billion loan from Russia over a period of three to four years at a very low interest rate: LIBOR plus thirty to fifty basis points. One may be intrigued by this move by the CBI. Its main purpose was to stop the flight of foreign capital from Iceland. Yet Prime Minister Geir Haarde revealed a secondary purpose: "We have not received the kind of support that we were requesting from our friends. So in a situation like that one has to look for new friends."[18]

Since the European Central Bank and the Federal Reserve did not install swap agreements with the CBI, Iceland changed

---

[18] As quoted in Kerry Capell, "The Stunning Collapse of Iceland,"

strategy. By asking for Russian help, Iceland was hoping to shock its former allies into rushing to its defense. Iceland had been home to an American military base for decades. Its strategic geopolitical position makes it attractive to both Russia and NATO. Asking Russia for a loan would not only trouble the consciences of Iceland's "friends" but also put pressure on them to grant a loan to Iceland in order to maintain their own military and political status vis-à-vis Russia.

In the end, the Russians backed out of the loan offer as the financial crisis reached their own borders. Although the Russian loan never materialized, the CBI was able to draw upon swap facilities granted by the central banks of Denmark and Norway for €200 million each. This foreign currency helped Iceland to import essential foodstuffs. On October 24 the IMF tentatively agreed to a loan of €1.57 billion. Following this loan, additional foreign loans were expected. However, the UK and the Netherlands halted the IMF loan, as they demanded that Landsbanki reimburse their depositors for their losses from investing in its subsidiary Icesave. Icesave was backed by the Icelandic deposit insurance fund, which had been increased to cover all domestic deposits *without limit.* According to the European Economic Area Treaty, the Icelandic government was obliged to guarantee at least the first €20,000 of *all* Icesave accounts. Since the Icelandic government had announced that it would not guarantee the foreign debts of the insolvent banks or provide deposit insurance, Dutch and British depositors stood to lose their deposits. Another reason why the British were taking a hard line was that the two Icelandic internet banks (Icesave and Kaupthing Edge) had attracted almost ten billion pounds of demand deposits away from UK banks. British banks were understandably not delighted with this competition and wanted their Icelandic competitors gone.

Loans from the Faroe Islands, Norway, and Poland (which had sent workers to the Iceland during boom times), were announced at the end of October and beginning of November,

---

*Bloomberg Businessweek* on msnbc.com (October 10, 2008).

giving Icelanders time and reserves to pay for imports. It was especially important to ensure that import trade remained robust, since Iceland imports almost all tradable goods except fish, dairy products, and meat.

Finally, on the nineteenth of November an agreement was reached with the IMF. The rescue package of $4.6 billion comprised $2.1 billion from the IMF and $2.5 billion of loans and currency swaps from Norway, Sweden, Finland and Denmark).

The following day, Iceland received an additional joint loan of $6.3 billion (€5 billion) from Germany, the United Kingdom, and the Netherlands to pay Icesave depositors in those countries. The additional debt imposed on the Icelandic government by this loan and the IMF loan package together amounted to almost $36,000 per Icelandic citizen, all to pay for the adventures of the banks.[19]

Only thanks to these rescue loans was it possible to stabilize the króna, secure essential imports, and gain enough time to restructure the economy. When the Icelandic interbank foreign exchange market reopened on December 2, the króna, which had fallen by more than fifty-eight percent during 2008, climbed to 153.3 to the euro. In January 2009 it finally stabilized. Technically the banking sector remained bankrupt, but it still functioned thanks to external credits, like a delinquent firm that honors old payments thanks to fresh credit.

It is by no means a coincidence that the markets lost confidence in the banks at a time when they were so vulnerable. Extreme levels of maturity mismatching ultimately caused the loss of confidence. The maturity mismatching increased the availability of long-term funds, thus artificially lowering long-term interest rates. The lower rates triggered malinvestments, such as those in the housing and aluminum smelting sectors. These malinvestments finally led to losses for the banks, damaging investor confidence and ending the rollover that was necessary to sustain them.

---

[19] Rowena Mason, "UK Treasury Lends Iceland £2.2 Billion to Compensate Icesave Customers," *The Telegraph* (November 20, 2008).

Chapter 7

# Why the Fed Could Save Its Bankers, But the CBI Could Not

On November 13, 2001, the Central Bank of Iceland, headed by Davíð Oddsson, issued a press release announcing it would effectively become a lender of last resort for the nation's financial community. While almost all central banks in the world implicitly undertake this role, Iceland's central bank explicitly committed itself to shouldering the weight of the banking system's bad decisions.

Commitment requires credibility. A central bank *usually* gains credibility as the lender of last resort through one oddity of its balance sheet: it can retire liabilities by creating more liabilities. As the central bank is that institution empowered to supply an area with money, it can settle claims against it by unilaterally increasing the money supply. Consequently, any debt obligations of the banking sector can easily, though not necessarily painlessly, be absorbed and nominally covered by the central bank.

The difficulty that arises with any lender of last resort, implicitly or explicitly guaranteed, is the problem of moral hazard. Privatizing benefits while socializing costs will always result in some degree of moral hazard. The lender of last resort skews the incentive structure, and a turn to riskier undertakings will result.

But what if a banking system is saddled with debt that is not denominated in domestic currency but is instead primarily foreign-denominated? In this case, the central monetary authority is limited in its power as a lender of last resort, as its monetary powers are limited to regulatory changes of the domestic banking sector (i.e., reserve requirements, capital adequacy ratios, etc.), open-market operations using its balance sheet assets to offset transactions, or inflating the domestic money supply. Assets denominated in foreign currencies become the lynchpin to the solvency of a banking system that is heavily indebted in foreign currencies.

In 2007, after ten years of growth, the big three Icelandic banks, Kaupthing, Glitnir, and Landsbanki, owned assets in excess of 1100 percent of Iceland's GDP, comprising nearly eighty percent of the island's total banking assets. An oversized and unviable banking model had developed.[1] The pretense under which this system developed—that a central bank stood ready and able to bail it out if it came under pressure—would be called into question as the crisis progressed.

Over the course of the year 2008, Iceland's stock of foreign exchange reserves was becoming critically low relative to the banking sector's liquidity demands. An even more pressing problem was that the flow of foreign exchange into the country was greatly diminished. The trade deficit that had developed in the early 2000s had remained steady throughout the decade. As the economy continually switched from a net exporter to a strong demander of imports, demand for the króna decreased. The trade deficit reached its peak in the fourth quarter of 2006, when the

---

[1]Buiter and Sibert, "The Icelandic Banking Crisis"; Jon Danielsson, "The

Icelandic economy was importing goods worth over sixty billion krónur more than it was exporting. This imbalance eased as the decade progressed, but by late 2008, the Icelandic economy was still importing over twenty-five billion krónur more in foreign goods (and foreign currency) than it was exporting.

The Central Bank of Iceland was in a difficult position, with scant foreign exchange reserves available to serve the needs of the banking system and with no chance of replenishing its coffers due to the persistent trade imbalance. It had committed to bailing out the banking sector if and when the need arose. The need had arisen, but the means were not available. The banking sector had taken on too many foreign-denominated liabilities that could not easily be satisfied by the supply of funds available. It was apparent that only outside support could save the financial system.

Early requests to various central banks for liquidity swaps mostly fell on deaf ears. Faced with the looming probability of a liquidity crisis within their own borders, foreign nations, even previously friendly ones, were less than anxious to lend money to Iceland. A plentiful supply of krónur was available to be swapped, but foreign nations were not keen on accepting the relatively unimportant currency in exchange for hard money that could be used to settle debt obligations. Finally, on May 16, 2008, the central banks of Sweden, Norway, and Denmark entered into bilateral euro/króna swap agreements. Each agreement allowed for up to €50 million on demand.

But €50 million was a drop in the bucket compared to the €70 billion of outstanding foreign-denominated liabilities that the Icelandic private banking system had accumulated.

The Bank of England was enthusiastic at first about an eventual swap agreement but turned decidedly colder as the year wore on. The European Central Bank was unwilling to enter into an agreement without an assessment by the IMF of Iceland's economy and the position of its banking system. The

---

First Casualty of the Crisis: Iceland," *VoxEU* (November 12, 2008).

IMF and the Fed were approached about helping Iceland, either by loaning money themselves or by assessing the economy's potential to see if other counterparties could be found.

Initial optimism about brokered swap agreements quickly dissipated, however, as the year progressed and the size and true nature of the Icelandic banking system became apparent. The Fed determined that the Icelandic banking system needed more aid than it could credibly commit to giving. Despite offering swap agreements to a plethora of other foreign central banks, it left the Central Bank of Iceland to fend for itself.

Lacking external support, the central bank attempted to expand its foreign exchange reserves on the open market by issuing short-term bills. Illiquid credit markets hindered this attempt, making any successful recapitalization via a bond issue all but impossible. Icelandic assets, which had until recently been in great demand, were now universally unwanted. Foreign countries had increasing credit problems of their own. They could not continue committing to provide for Iceland.

By October, the CBI had drawn on its Nordic euro swap lines to the order of €40 million. These friendly nations extended the swap agreements to year-end 2009, and it was expected that this would provide sustained relief for the central bank.

But by October 9 the situation had deteriorated to the point where the CBI issued a statement to the public reiterating that the economy was sound and that the central bank was committed to maintaining a solid credit rating. This commitment had been evidenced just days earlier, when the CBI negotiated its €4 billion Russian loan.

International opposition to the Russian bailout was apparent, and many countries that had previously given Iceland the cold shoulder now warmed to the idea of a bailout. The Russian loan soon fell through as the IMF worked to negotiate a stand-by arrangement (SBA).

The Icelandic government was able to reach the SBA *ad referendum* with the IMF on October 24, 2008 allowing for approximately $2.2 billion to be made available for two years. The IMF would disburse $830 million immediately, with the remainder spread over the remaining life of the agreement. On November 19, 2008, the agreement was finalized and the first payment was made. The IMF later extended the SBA to May 31, 2011.

This agreement did much to stem the tide of insolvency that the CBI was facing in the short term. However, it did little to relieve the longer-term problems of the Icelandic economy. The badly depreciated exchange rate put Iceland in danger of being cut off from imports it desperately needed: food, pharmaceuticals, and oil.

The crisis strained friendships. Previously close allies ignored Iceland's initial pleas for help.[2]

It was only with some foreign help that the króna was stabilized at the beginning of January 2009. The CBI received high-quality assets and thereby increased the average quality of the assets backing its currency, commencing a period of "qualitative enhancement."[3] New foreign exchange reserves were used to pay for imports and to begin restoring confidence in the currency. The króna stabilized, and inflation rates moderated throughout the spring of 2009. As the average quality of the assets backing the currency increased due to foreign loans providing higher-

---

[2] Jónsson, *Why Iceland?* pp. 138, 188.

[3] Qualitative enhancement consists in the improvement of the average quality of assets backing a currency. Qualitative enhancement is, thus, the opposite of qualitative easing. It can be achieved while the balance sheet total is changing by adding higher-quality assets or liquidating lower quality ones, or with a constant balance sheet total by selling lower quality assets and buying higher quality assets. The term *qualitative easing*, which denotes a new form of monetary policy used heavily during the recession following the liquidity crisis of 2008 distinct from the more well-known quantitative easing, was coined by Philipp Bagus and Markus H. Schiml ("New Modes of Monetary Policy: Qualitative Easing by the Fed," *Economic Affairs* 29, no. 2 [2009]: pp. 81–93) and later developed by Philipp Bagus and David Howden ("Qualitative Easing in Support of a Tumbling Financial System: A Look at the Eurosystem's Recent Balance Sheet Policies," *Economic Affairs* 29, no. 4 [2009]: pp. 60–65; "The Federal Reserve and Eurosystem's Balance Sheet Policies During the Financial Crisis: A Comparative Analysis," *Romanian Economic and Business Review* 4, no. 3 [2009]: pp. 165–85).

quality liquidity, the quality of the króna increased.

The explicit commitment of the Central Bank of Iceland to act as the lender of last resort had endangered the stability of the nation. While the CBI was capitalized well enough in terms of foreign assets relative to its own foreign-denominated liabilities to weather any storms from adverse exchange rate movements, once it shouldered the burden of the private banking sector's liabilities, the situation changed starkly. In Figure 17, we can see that throughout 2007–08, the CBI was covering foreign-denominated liabilities amounting to between *3,000 and 4,000 times* its foreign-denominated asset base. Since the private banking sector's liabilities had effectively become CBI liabilities, regardless of their denomination, we must assess the financial position of the central bank in light of these obligations. The huge foreign indebtedness of the domestic banking sector weighed heavily on the central bank, reducing the ratio of foreign assets to liabilities to a *mere 4–6 percent.*[4]

This ratio peaked in August 2008 as the CBI bought foreign reserves in order to increase its liquidity. The International Monetary Fund increased Icelandic Special Drawing Rights (SDR) by almost fifteen billion krónur, providing support to the dwindling foreign exchange reserves of the CBI.[6] While this spike

---

[4] Accounting for these banking obligations, the Central Bank of Iceland was insolvent on its balance sheet, a rare situation for a central bank to find itself in, as analyzed in Maxwell J. Fry ("Can Central Banks Go Bust?" *The Manchester School of Economics and Social Studies* 60 [Supplement 1992]: pp. 85–98) and Willem H. Buiter ("Can Central Banks Go Broke?" *Centre for Economic Policy Research Policy Insight* no. 24 [May 2008]).

[5] Calculated as the sum of foreign-denominated assets (including gold) divided by total foreign liabilities.

[6] Positive equity is essential for a central bank to retain its independence from its central government. The risk of recapitalization may entail a sacrifice in this independence, as the fiscal authority provides the central bank with new capital. While previous work has focused on a central bank's own fiscal authority recapitalizing it (Claudio Borio and Piti Disyatat, "Unconventional Monetary Policies: An Appraisal," *The Manchester School* 78 [September 2010]: pp. 53–89; Olivier Jeanne and Lars Svensson, "Credible Commitment to Optimal Escape from a Liquidity Trap: The Role of the Balance Sheet

## Why the Fed Could Save Its Bankers, But the CBI Could Not 101

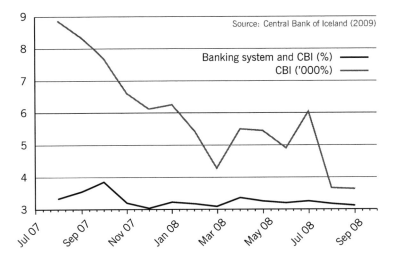

**Figure 17:** Central Bank of Iceland liquidity ratio (August 2007–September 2009).[5]

may have given the impression that the CBI had abundant, or at least sufficient, foreign assets to fund its import obligations, in fact the effect of the foreign asset infusions was short-lived. They did at least succeed in stabilizing the currency.

Not only did the CBI lack sufficient liquidity to cover the banking system's foreign-denominated debts, it also lacked liquidity of an applicable maturity. Figure 18 shows the funding gaps across different maturities of the Icelandic debt market, including both liabilities of the Central Bank of Iceland and liabilities of the big three financial institutions. Positive funding gaps imply an excess of liabilities without corresponding assets with which to fund them.

The heavy maturity mismatch of the financial system becomes evident. There were ample assets of long maturity, both

---

of an Independent Central Bank," *American Economic Review* 97, no. 1 [2007]: pp. 474–490), the Icelandic case is unique as the Icelandic government lacked the ability to do this. Instead, neighboring Nordic countries and the IMF provided the loans and capital necessary for continued operations. The effects of these foreign interventions on the CBI's independence remain to be seen.

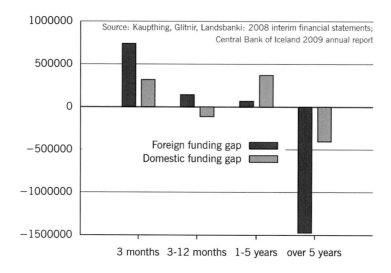

**Figure 18**: Funding gaps, Central Bank of Iceland and big three banks combined (million krónur).

in krónur and in foreign funds. As a consequence of borrowing short and investing long, there were 1.5 trillion krónur ($210 billion) more long-term assets maturing than there were long-term liabilities in need of funding. The banking system would unfortunately require its liquidity much sooner than the minimum five years that it would have to wait for these long-term assets to mature. In the meantime, these long-term ventures were funded by taking advantage of the low interest rates offered by short-term debt, especially for maturities of under three months. A burgeoning gap of 740 billion krónur ($10.5 billion) of unfunded short-term liabilities sat on the financial system's balance sheet, requiring that willing savers continually roll over new funds into it.

The banking system relied on a continual flow of short-term funding, especially foreign funding, but the central bank had very little funding to offer, and the meager supplies it did have would not be available until several years in the future. A short-term liquidity constraint brought the banking system to insolvency. Short-term loans proffered by the international community alleviated this liquidity crunch but failed to provide a lasting solution. The banking system will solve this liquidity problem only when it rematches its debt obligations to its funding assets.

Today the central bank has essentially no net foreign reserves. Provided that exchange rate volatility remains low, this causes no significant problem. The short-term liquidity constraint is not binding, as foreign lending to Icelandic banks is not pressingly low and foreign investors' future purchasing power guarded by a stable exchange rate. However, today's underfunded banking system is no improvement on the old unsustainable system. If there is another liquidity crisis Iceland will find itself in an even more perilous position than it did in late 2008, as it lacks any ability to fund imports with non-króna-denominated liabilities.

The seemingly innocuous promise that the Central Bank of Iceland made in 2001 to act as the lender of last resort contributed to the downfall of Iceland's banking sector, of its central bank, of its national finances and, eventually, of its government. This promise lulled the banks into taking on increasing levels of foreign indebtedness and increasingly risky foreign liabilities, secured by the word of the Central Bank of Iceland that it would aid them when a liquidity crunch came. This was to be the undoing of the CBI, as it lacked sufficient resources to carry out such a rescue. It was capitalized more than well enough to sustain its own operations, but the sheer size and international scope of the lending operations of the Icelandic banking sector, led by the big three banks, made it impossible for the CBI to offer them meaningful aid.

Chapter 8

# The Necessary Restructuring

Three aspects of Icelandic life need to return to normal for the economy to regain its footing and climb out of its pit.

Malinvestments—those misdirected resources and entrepreneurial errors—need to be liquidated. Prolonging their existence prevents the economy from moving production and consumption patterns to those that are conducive to long-term growth.

An oversized financial sector is not necessary for the country, nor is it healthy. It has removed resources from those areas where Iceland has a real competitive advantage. The financial sector needs to be allowed to shrink down to the size required by Iceland's economy.

Lastly, the consumption-led boom bred a new type of Icelander. The inflationary economy of the boom years increased the time preference of the nation. Icelanders need to regain their traditional prudence about credit and spending. As Howden[1] remarks of the recovery process necessary for ailing economies,

---
[1] Howden, "Knowledge Shifts," p. 179.

A healthy recovery phase, then, will be one characterized by an allowance for entrepreneurs to replace the skills learned in the previous expansionary financial environment with the skills needed for the maintenance of the production structure. To the extent that entrepreneurs are inhibited from completing this necessary transition, a healthy recovery phase will be delayed.

Allowing these three areas to return to normal will be a painful but a wholly necessary requisite for recovery. Delaying this outcome, whether via further inflation, exchange rate controls or manipulations, bailouts, or state guarantees, will prolong Iceland's misery.

### Resource Adjustment

Credit expansion led to an artificially lengthened productive structure. This usually implies an increase in the production of capital goods, as signaled by the relative profitability increase at those orders of production further from their final.

During Iceland's boom, capital shifted away from the previous mainstays in the economy, fishing and maritime products. These traditional industries were gradually eroded in favor of more capital-intensive production processes. A housing boom occurred which now leaves the island with a glut of inventory in search of homeowners or renters. The increased aluminum smelting capacity to capitalize on Iceland's vast supply of cheap electricity now searches for profitable use. Investors started a plethora of capital-intensive industries and businesses over the past decade, at the expense of the mundane but stable industries in which Icelanders have historically specialized.

These specific malinvestments will prove difficult, though not impossible, to rectify. The process will involve two steps—both somewhat painful.

First, overconsumption during the boom led to a misallocation of goods. The crisis forced many to rethink their previously prolific spending. Many Icelanders were unable and unwilling to keep paying for cars bought with foreign-denominated loans. They defaulted on their automobile loans, and a surplus of used cars stormed the market at low prices. HEKLA, a seventy-four-year-old car importer and dealer in Iceland, constructed a database of used vehicles to help clear the market. With purchase prices attractive internationally due to the severely devalued króna, buyers from the Faroe Islands, Norway, Denmark, Sweden, and Germany rushed to purchase cars that cost comparatively little.[2] Though it has no automobile production facilities, Iceland has become an exporter of cars.

The shedding of excess consumers' goods, such as the cars bought during the boom, must continue until the economy regains stability. Reducing the excess supply of used consumers' goods will allow prices for new goods to stabilize. Besides shedding the excess consumers' goods from the economy, these exports will also serve an additional purpose. Foreign buyers who pay in foreign currency will provide a much-needed source of foreign exchange to cover the previously incurred debts. Foreign buyers who pay in Icelandic krónur will need, in most instances, to purchase these krónur on the open market, thus providing demand to support Iceland's currency.

Second, entrepreneurs will need to redirect physical capital resources to areas of the economy in need. During the boom years, physical resources were redirected away from the productive maritime-based economy into construction. Depreciated fishing fleets will need to be repaired or built anew to reverse this resource shift. These specific malinvestments will prove difficult, but not impossible, to rectify.

This move back to a more traditional economy has been met with some obstacles. On July 10, 2009, the Minister of Fisheries announced the fishing quotas for the 2009–2010 fishing year. The total quota for haddock was reduced by almost fifty percent

---

[2]HEKLA was so eager to profit from these exports that it offered to cover the shipping costs for any buyers of its used vehicles. Used cars proved to be one source of necessary foreign income during the collapse.

(30,000 tonnes) and the cod quota was reduced by eight percent (12,500 tonnes).[3] This reduction could not have come at a worse time, as Iceland needs to obtain foreign currency via its exports to help it emerge from recession.

Other recent events have brought some improvement. On January 29, 2010, the capelin quota was increased to 130,000 tonnes. Of this total, the Minister of Fisheries will allocate over 97,000 tonnes to the Icelandic fishing fleet, with the remainder auctioned to foreigners.[4] The Icelandic allocation promotes a return to a traditional economy led by maritime products, which will eventually increase exports. The quota allocated to foreigners will bring an immediate inflow of foreign exchange to ease the funding shortfall.

Labor will be a particularly time-consuming resource to shift. Because the distribution of the labor force among different industries underwent significant changes during the boom, a reassignment of the workforce will be necessary to employ the physical resources that entrepreneurs shifted away from previously unprofitable businesses and industries. Labor's primary defining feature as a resource, nonspecificity, will turn out to be its greatest advantage *and* disadvantage in this process.

On the one hand, other physical resources will be only suitable to specific production processes. Newly produced condominiums, for example, cannot easily be diverted to satisfy the increased requirement for fish processing capacity. Bankers' software programs, purchased to organize, track, and manage ballooning loan portfolios during the boom, cannot be used for any other purpose except that specific one. In fact, all physical capital has some degree of specificity. It is more suited to one production process rather than another. Labor, in contrast, is often a less specific input. Individuals can be reassigned to different production processes relatively easily.

A worker has the capacity to think for himself, undergo training, and change the ends towards which his labor may be

---

[3]Central Bank of Iceland, *Monetary Bulletin* 11, no. 4 (2009), p. 63.
[4]Central Bank of Iceland, *Monetary Bulletin* 12, no. 2 (2010), p. 82.

applied. While this is labor's distinct advantage, guaranteeing that labor always has the possibility to be utilized, it also poses difficulties. While other physical resources can be instantly reassigned provided that a suitable alternative use is available which they are suited to fulfill, labor will almost certainly require a period of time as its capabilities are altered. Training and reeducation time, in addition to the more commonly identified job search time, will be necessary to match employees to newly minted positions. A fisherman-turned-banker who Michael Lewis interviewed during Iceland's boom illustrates the specific problem that labor runs into. The fisherman lamented, "I think it is easier to take someone in the fishing industry and teach him about currency trading than to take someone from the banking industry and teach them how to fish".[5]

Anything that delays the reassignment of labor to more productive uses will increase the time until the economy returns to normal. Unemployment insurance decreases the incentive for the newly unemployed to seek reemployment in more profitable areas of the economy. Icelandic unemployment compensation is both generous and long lasting. It is available to anyone between the ages of sixteen and sixty-nine, and the sole requirement is that the worker has undertaken at least ten weeks of insured employment within the previous twelve-month period. Benefits amount to anywhere from 1,362 to 5,446 krónur per day.[6] Unemployment insurance can be continued, provided that the recipient works no more than two days a week. Coverage continues for a maximum period of three years.

These benefits have resulted in a sharp decline in the number of labor hours worked by the average Icelander during the crisis. While other countries have suffered sudden increases in unemployment during the past few years, Iceland's true situation has

---

[5]Lewis, "Wall Street on the Tundra."

[6]In 2008, this amounted to a weekly unemployment insurance payment of between $112 and $446. By way of comparison, a comparable European country, Ireland, had a maximum unemployment insurance payment of $289 per week for a maximum duration of fifteen months.

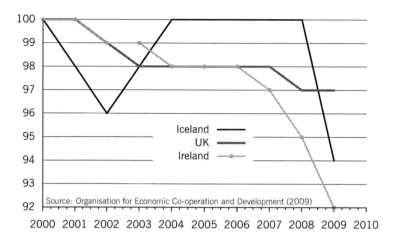

**Figure 19:** Average annual hours worked per employee (2000 = 100)

been somewhat masked by a peculiarity of the Icelandic labor market. Despite the appearance of an endless party during the boom-years, it was the norm that Icelanders worked two jobs to make ends meet. As a result, unemployment during the bust has been understated. Many people have lost one of their two jobs but still have the other; thus, the official unemployment statistics do not count them. A better measure of the decline in employment is the number of labor hours worked by the average citizen (Figure 19).

At the boom's peak, the average Icelander was working 1,822 hours per year. By 2009 this had declined to just over 1,717 hours, nearly a six percent decline. This decline in hours worked has been more rapid in Iceland than in Europe's other problem child, Ireland, and has made the decline in hours worked in Britain look paltry in comparison. Of the Icelanders registered as unemployed in 2009, eighty-five percent of them claim to have lost their job in October, just after the collapse of the financial system.[7]

---

[7] Iceland Review, "Salary Cuts for 14 Percent of Wage Earners" (January 14, 2009).

Anything that hinders either the labor, goods, or financial markets from adjusting will prolong the pain of the Icelandic population. Flexibility is essential to allow factors to shift from the areas where they were malinvested to the areas where they can be most profitably used. A more flexible labor market, by reducing regulations and incentives not to work (i.e., unemployment insurance), would aid recovery by enticing workers to return to traditional industries more quickly.

## Shrinking the Financial Sector

The shift away from the then relatively unprofitable real sectors of the economy (i.e., production-based sectors) and into the banking and, eventually, finance sectors may have been the most apparent event of the boom, and the reversal of this shift is the most apparent event of the current bust.

While the prospect of a whole industry engulfed in layoffs, empty offices, foreclosed branches, and a deteriorating reputation may seem unfortunate, we must realize that it is an unavoidable step on the long road to recovery. The source of the crisis is, after all, the promotion of an oversized and unsustainable financial sector, reliant on artificially reduced interest rates to remain profitable.

The shift has already largely occurred. While the physical resource shift that is necessary to shrink the sheer size of this behemoth of an industry will take some time — bankers need to be retrained for new jobs, bank offices need to be refurbished for new uses — the movement of financial capital out of the financial sector has taken place to a large extent already. Bank share prices have already collapsed, financial companies have gone bust, and previously soaring profits and bonuses have been reduced or eliminated. Iceland's króna fell by more than fifty-eight percent during 2008 before stabilizing. In the short term there was considerable pain, but the long-term signal could not have been clearer.

The short-term pain was mainly from skyrocketing prices for imports — imports that the economy had come to rely on as the trade deficit mushroomed. Though it must have seemed disastrous to many, this rise in prices should have been welcomed as a clear signal that Iceland's economy had reached a tipping point. While the increase in real prices forced painful changes, it also signaled Iceland's new economic advantage. A cheaper króna made Icelandic exports relatively cheap for foreign countries, thus bolstering demand for these goods. It should be apparent by now that the real problem since the value of the króna stabilized at its new lower value has not been the relative increase in the price of imports to the country; the problem has been the lack of productive capacity to produce goods for export and capitalize on the new comparative advantage.

As the exchange rate resumed a position aligned with Iceland's comparative advantage—exporting marine-based or energy-intensive products to the world—it became clear that there was no available excess capacity to meet this demand quickly. Financial assets quickly and effortlessly adjusted downward in price to reflect the reality of the situation, but real assets were slower to grow. If productive capacity had the characteristic of being instantly and effortlessly scalable, Iceland could have capitalized on the newly adjusted financial prices with little net disruption to the Icelandic financial landscape.

One significant feature of the government's actions during the bust was its concerted effort to maintain the primacy of the financial sector. As the big three Icelandic banks, Kaupthing, Glitnir, and Landsbanki, neared or entered bankruptcy in late 2008 it should have been taken as a clear signal that financial assets had been misdirected previously and could be more productive in alternative uses. But a concerted effort was made to save these banks; they were nationalized, and they continue to operate.

The result was a prohibition of the natural response to the crisis. The financial sector was not allowed to shrink to the extent that was necessary for sustainability. Consequently, the real productive economy has not been able to expand to the extent necessary to benefit from the advantageous exchange rate depreciation.

While resources invested in industries and firms that produce goods for export would have realized an instant profit at the prevailing exchange rates, those resources that were directed towards the banking sector were met with continued losses or, as a best-case scenario, an uncertain future. Directing resources into the banking sector not only prolongs the life of this unsustainable aspect of the Icelandic economy, but also makes those resources unavailable to Iceland's export-based production sectors.

In choosing to support the banking and financial sectors, the government weighed the advantages of easing short-term pain more heavily than the disadvantages of constraining long-term growth. Many will be quick to point out that Iceland's economy, at least in its present state, relies on its financial industry. Whether this ever should have been the case can be answered in the negative. The future will require a pint-sized banking sector. How much smaller the Icelandic banking sector needs to get in order to become sustainable again remains to be seen.

Chapter 9

# Concluding Remarks

The spectacular collapse of the Icelandic economy has attracted much interest. Often it is asserted that speculators or free-market reforms caused the downturn. Nothing could be farther from the truth.

Iceland is far from being a libertarian paradise. Despite former Prime Minister (and later CBI chairman) Davíð Oddsson's free-market rhetoric and his affection for the Thatcher and Reagan eras, Iceland is close to the Scandinavian model of the welfare state. In 2007, its fiscal burden was ninth highest among nations in the OECD (41.4 percent of GDP, higher than both Germany and France).

Although there was deregulation and privatization of the banking sector, the Icelandic banking sector was very far from being a free market. It is true that banks could act freely, but they operated within a framework of government-created incentives, and it was these incentives that caused a business cycle. In fact, Iceland is a perfect example of an economic collapse caused by a national fiat paper money. Fiat paper money has nothing to do with free-market money. The privilege of fractional reserve banking (i.e., appropriating deposited money and engaging in credit expansion) violates a depositor's property rights. The Central Bank of Iceland directed the credit expansion, expanded the monetary base, and assumed the role of an explicit lender of last resort. Central banking is one of the last bastions of government planning and socialism.[1]

While central banks in other developed nations at least nominally enjoy independence from the government that has granted their monopoly, in Iceland there was no doubt that the CBI was always a manifestation of political forces. Two of its three governors were direct political appointees. Davíð Oddsson, who presided over the CBI during its dramatic fall from grace, had previously been the Prime Minister of the nation (he was also not an economist but a lawyer by training). When it was apparent that the Central Bank had allowed the country's finances to fall into a catastrophic state, the new Prime Minister, Johanna Sigurdottir, ousted Oddsson. The lack of a strong rule of law constraining politicians was never bluntly exposed: "Johanna Sigurdottir understood that she could not sack Davíð Oddsson outright; she could, however, make it clear that if he did not go of his own free will, she could rush through a law stipulating, for example, that the governor of the central bank had to have economic training."[2]

The existence of a central bank that is prepared to help troubled banks greatly encourages credit expansion and maturity mismatching.[3] The CBI was no more an advocate of a free market than other central banks are. It simply followed the credit expansion directed by the rest of the central banks, under the illusion that the artificial reduction of interest rates would be beneficial to the coordination of the economy. As a roller-over of last resort the CBI encouraged maturity mismatching, which was one of the two ingredients in the explosive cocktail that would blow up Iceland's financial sector. The other main ingredient,

---

[1]Huerta de Soto, *Money, Bank Credit and Economic Cycles*, p. xxii.  [2]Boyes, *Meltdown Iceland*, pp. 197–98.  [3]Bagus, "Austrian Business Cycle Theory."

currency mismatching, was encouraged by the illusion that currency swaps could protect against a rollover stoppage in the international wholesale markets.

It was not understood that credit expansion itself leads to this rollover stoppage. As credit expansion engenders malinvestment, an unsustainable situation develops. The economy becomes increasingly fragile. When currency mismatching is coupled with maturity mismatching—and a credit expansion relying on demand deposits is by definition maturity mismatching—even a relatively small disruption of liquidity will make the house of cards come toppling down. The collapse of Lehman Brothers in late 2008 did not cause the demise of Iceland's economy; it simply exposed the errors that investors had made earlier.

The two primary factors exacerbated the maturity mismatch. First, the Central Bank of Iceland's easy monetary policy fueled the move to short-term debt durations. As monetary policy primarily took effect at the short end of the yield curve, short rates were driven lower than the long rates. Because the money supply was continually expanding, short-term borrowing could be continually rolled over. Bankers and entrepreneurs could effortlessly profit by borrowing at artificially low short-term rates while investing in longer-term projects. When short-term credit disappeared, a bust swiftly ensued that exposed the unprofitability of these longer-term investment projects (primarily housing and aluminum smelting). The second factor that exacerbated the maturity mismatch was artificially low interest rates worldwide, which enabled Icelanders to borrow at further low interest rates. It became common to borrow sums denominated in Japanese yen, Swiss francs, euros, and U.S. dollars. This borrowing was not problematic as long as the króna maintained its value (indeed, increased in value), but the sharp drop in the value of the króna in 2008 quickly ended the foreign investment.

Entrepreneurs undertake all foreign-denominated investments with a degree of currency rate risk. As floating rates may adjust during the time between when a contract is struck and when it is fully paid, exchange rate movements can significantly alter the final repayment amount. Entrepreneurs factor for this added risk premium, and it is a disincentive to borrow excessively in a foreign currency. Icelanders seemed to ignore this risk factor during the boom, undertaking unnerving amounts of foreign-denominated debts while offsetting them with relatively few foreign assets or revenues.

The extreme degree of currency mismatching that the Icelandic banks engaged in can be partly explained by two factors.

First, many investors—both Icelandic and foreign—saw the International Monetary Fund as being capable of providing stability. With this implicit assurance in place, currency investors could sleep well knowing that Iceland had a good chance of being aided when or if its economy finally faltered.

Second, the Central Bank of Iceland provided an additional guarantee in 2001 when it explicitly promised to act as the lender of last resort. Secure in the knowledge that investments that went south would be covered, investors threw due diligence out the window and behaved with irrational exuberance. Banks could not compete with each other without taking on ever-riskier investments. Because borrowing in low-interest-rate foreign currencies added to profitability, banks faced a dilemma: either partake in the boom, regardless of how unsustainable it seems, or be driven out of business by your counterparts who do participate in it. Yet while the CBI was capitalized well enough in comparison to the pre-boom Icelandic banking system to function should the recession not subside quickly, it was woefully undercapitalized to assume a position of lender of last resort for the now much larger banking industry. More importantly, the CBI, which existed in part to combat insolvency scenarios, faced insolvency itself as it was overwhelmed by the liabilities of the private banking industry. Since it had explicitly pledged its support, the Central Bank was on the hook for any private sector losses.

Some other commentators have remarked that Iceland was an innocent victim. Had a global credit crunch not restricted liquidity its banking system could remain largely intact today.

IMF mission chief to Iceland Mark Flanagan said as much in a recent interview:

> [G]iven the large financial shock that ultimately hit not only Iceland, [sic] but the entire world, it would probably not have been possible to prevent the crisis in Iceland itself. And we need to think deeply about why this happened, and if more could have been done to prevent it, to make sure it never happens again.[4]

Nothing could be further from the truth. To believe that Iceland was an innocent bystander of the liquidity crisis of late 2008 would be to ignore Iceland's economic policies over the previous decade, which had fostered an oversized, indebted, and mismatched banking system.

The Icelandic crisis was wholly avoidable. Nothing was sprung upon the economy without warning. Actions with unintended consequences, both by Icelandic policymakers and by the international community, resulted in one of the largest economic busts to disrupt a developed economy. The effects have been widespread. The economy has undergone drastic changes, and will need to go through many more if recovery is to strengthen. The Icelandic language carries some marks of the crisis. "Two thousand seven," the last year of good times to roll by prior to the collapse, is now used as an adjective to describe excess. Icelanders now dismiss someone buying a new expensive car, throwing a luxurious party or taking an exotic vacation as being "so two thousand seven." "Kreppa," an Icelandic word usually used to denote "in a pinch" or "to get into a scrape," is now synonymous with the financial crisis.[5]

The temptation for Iceland to join the European Monetary Union has proven strong in the aftermath of the worst financial crisis of the 21$^{st}$ century. The Icelandic public's resolution against joining the European Union has strengthened over the

---

[4] As quoted in Andersen, "Iceland Gets Help."
[5] "Kreppanomics," *The Economist* (October 9, 2008).

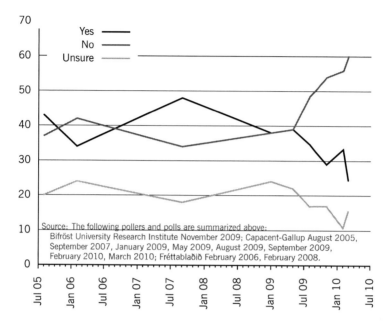

**Figure 20**: Public Opinion on Icelandic accession to the EU (August 2005–February 2010)

past five years, and especially since the onset of the crisis. Figure 20 shows a compilation of various public polls inquiring whether Iceland should join the EU. Despite this widespread opposition among voters, the *Althing* voted on July 16, 2009 in favor of accession talks with the Union.[6] The Icelandic government lodged a formal application to join the European Union on the same date, with official negotiations beginning on July 27, 2010.

It is notable that Iceland already enjoys being a member of the EU's single market (since 1994), and is a member of the Schengan Area (since 2001) which removes all border controls between member states. Opposition to joining both the EU and the Eurozone remained strong throughout the boom. Former Prime Minister Geir Haarde affirmed this hesitation to join the

---

[6]Of sixty-three parliamentary votes cast, thirty-three were in favor of EU accession talks, twenty-eight against, and two abstentions (EurActiv, "Iceland's Parliament Votes in Favour of EU Talks" [July 17, 2009].

European Union as recently as March 31, 2006 at a speech hosted by the University of Iceland, "Our policy is not to join in the foreseeable future. We are not even exploring membership."[7] The European Union has made it clear that admittance to the Economic and Monetary Union (EMU), with its subsequent adoption of the euro, will not be possible without first ascending to full EU membership. While many Icelanders today see a growing attractiveness to euro adoption, few want the bureaucratic entanglements that will go along with EU membership.

Pressure to join the EU, with or without euro currency adoption has been waxing. The Social Democrat Prime Minister Jóhanna Sigurðardóttir has pushed for euro adoption as a response to the crisis's aftermath. Iceland's Business Minister, Gylfi Magnusson, favors EU membership as a way to stabilize the country's currency, "The main benefits of EU membership at the moment would be the possibility of joining the exchange rate mechanism, and eventually adopting the euro."[8] One other "senior Icelandic official" has been quoted as saying, "The krona [sic] is dead. We need a new currency. The only serious option is the euro."[9] While euro-adoption provides a quick fix to the króna problem, joining the European Union, as the EU has made clear will be a necessary requirement for membership in the currency union, brings less clear advantages.

We may at this point question what benefit EU membership would bring that is not already forthcoming under inclusion in the European Economic Area. "EEA membership has been good for Iceland, which pays relatively little into EU funds, and runs its own farm and fish policies (it also escapes EU laws banning whaling)."[10] Indeed, as Iceland's Left-Green Political party has recently noted, "EU-membership would diminish the

---

[7] As quoted in Hjörtur J. Guðmundsson, "Slashing the Rumors: Iceland is Far From Adopting the Euro," *TEAM Europe* (May 5, 2006).

[8] As quoted in BBC News, "Iceland Moves Towards Joining EU" (July 16, 2009).

[9] As quoted in Ian Traynor, "Iceland to be Fast-Tracked into the EU," *The Guardian* (January 30, 2009).

[10] "Iceland Hunts the Euro," *The Economist* (January 22, 2009).

independence of Iceland even more than the EEA Agreement does and jeopardize Iceland's control over its resources."[11] European Commissioner for Economic and Financial Affairs Olli Rehn has confirmed that Iceland's access to its resources may be jeopardized, noting that although EU accession would be relatively easy for Iceland (potentially requiring less than one year of negotiations), it would not get any special treatment. Fishing quotas and whaling would likely be tough issues for Iceland to control during such negotiations. Given that the seafood industry accounts for thirty-seven percent of Iceland's exports, and employs eight percent of the work force, having one of their key natural resources fall under the sway of the EU's Common Fisheries Policy creates a cause for concern for the small island nation.[12]

In fact, while Rehn and other Europhiles encourage Iceland's accession to the EU, it is difficult to find any well-placed rationale. As Rehn himself recently commented about Iceland's admittance, "It is one of the oldest democracies in the world and its strategic and economic positions would be an asset to the EU."[13] It is difficult to say, to which exact economic positions Rehn refers. The country has, after all, just suffered the worst economic collapse of the 21$^{st}$ century, with a lasting recovery still uncertain. Iceland possesses two significant assets that are of strategic interest to the EU. First are rich fishing grounds that could be integrated into the EU's Common Fisheries Policy

---

[11] As quoted in Francesco Rossi, "Iceland's Icesave Referendum: A Possible Outcome Suggested by Electoral Perspective," Working paper (2010), p. 15.

[12] Leo Cendrowicz, "Iceland's Urgent Bid to Join the E.U.," *Time* (July 17, 2009).

[13] As quoted in Traynor, "Iceland to be Fast-Tracked." Given the tenuous reasons promoting Icelandic membership in the European Union now coming forward, the words of Gier Haarde from almost five years ago are proving prescient, "[S]ince in Iceland the interest in joining the EU has rather decreased than increased in recent years, those in favour have found themselves in a growing despair to get Iceland into the union. As a consequence they try to use every imaginable and unimaginable opportunity to raise the EU issue, with catastrophic results" (as quoted in Guðmundsson, "Slashing the Rumors").

for its own gain. Second is its strategic location in the North Atlantic—an aspect that has been exploited by foreign nations throughout Iceland's history for military purposes. It is not immediately clear what advantages Iceland would gain by sacrificing either of these resources for EU admittance. Indeed, as former Prime Minister and then-chairman of the CBI Davíð Oddsson cautioned during an October seventeenth 2008 interview with the *Wall Street Journal*, "[i]f we were tied to the euro, ... we would just have to succumb to the laws of Germany and France."

More importantly, it is not immediately clear that admittance to the European Union, or adoption of the euro currency, would have staved off Iceland's current woes. Other periphery EU countries suffered booms like Iceland, and still find themselves in the midst of recovery. The PIIGS countries—Portugal, Ireland, Italy, Greece and Spain—were not immune to these causes. Iceland may have suffered at the hands of an overexuberant central bank, but this factor would not be removed by sacrificing monetary decisions to the ECB in Frankfurt. In fact, for several years leading up to its crisis, the Central Bank of Iceland modeled its liquidity rules on those of the ECB. We may say that they were only *largely* modeled after the ECB because for quite a while the Icelandic Rules were more stringent than those of the ECB.[14] The CBI only slackened these rules in the late stages of the boom in an attempt to resemble those that existed within the ECB's jurisdiction (in terms of collateral requirements, for example). The prolific printing of money by the ECB flowed into Iceland primarily by a reduction in the risk premium that investors were willing to place on Icelandic borrowing. Joining the common currency area would, if anything, increase the ease at which Frankfurt's easy credit policy would be transferred to Reykjavík.

Nor is it clear that the European Union would be any more forthcoming with emergency funds when the time arose to combat the crisis. The Greek situation proved to be a difficult political fix in the early months of 2010. At the end of the day, the EU

---

[14]Friðriksson, "The Banking Crisis," p. 7.

was not alone in bailing out the indebted Greeks. The IMF was also called in to provide emergency loans. Although a plausible fix for the crisis at hand, membership in the EU has a less than stellar historical record over the past few years at dealing with crises in its existing member states. Nor is it readily apparent that the EU has the funds to handle its existing crises, let alone a fresh one in the North Atlantic.

Iceland's fate has already been sealed. An unsustainable boom must now give rise to a cleansing recession to clean the imbalances created over the past decade out of the system. Only then may a return to sustainable recovery, and growth, begin. With Iceland's short-term sustainability more or less provided through by the emergency loans and swap agreements, the longer-term goal of growth must be centered upon. Addressing the monetary factors that enabled such a disproportionately sized banking system to develop is the crux of the road to recovery. The Icelandic tragedy would not have been possible in a free monetary and financial system. Commentators who have charged that "free-market reforms" should shoulder the burden of blame for the crisis must identify a much different cause. Peter Gumbel's December 2008 assessment, written for CNN, that Iceland had become a "giant hedge fund" as a result of former Prime Minister Davíð Oddsson's reforms misses a critical point. The reason that a tiny island country could become a major player in global finance was due to monetary factors. Easy money policies at home and abroad, as well as political guarantees (the effective socialization of losses) perverted the incentive structure of the previously reserved nation. The political nature of Icelandic monetary policy is now evident. A banking system that was given the legal privilege of employing fractional reserves reared a nation of prolific borrowers and excessive risk takers.

Under a 100 percent commodity standard (gold, for example), credit expansion is impossible by definition. If banks have to honor time-tested legal principles and maintain 100-percent reserves on their demand deposits, they cannot create money out of thin air. Even a fractional reserve gold standard like the monetary system that prevailed before the First World War would have limited the credit expansion.

More importantly, the explosive ingredient of currency mismatching would have been eliminated. If the world had been on a gold standard, currency mismatching and its dangers would have been impossible. Iceland could not have indebted itself massively in the short-term in its domestic currency or in mismatching foreign currencies, as both currencies would have been gold. Banks would have stayed solvent. Even if an individual bank had gotten into trouble, its small size would have made the economic repercussions manageable if a market-based capital injection became necessary. Lending would have been constrained, both in magnitude and in counterparty. There would have been no stock market boom or housing boom.

Foreign exchange rates would have been fixed according to the gold content of the currencies. The Icelandic gold króna would have fluctuated only negligibly relative to the other gold currencies. Small fluctuations would trigger opposite gold flows, which would arbitrage the gold currencies into line with their gold content. Consequently, Iceland would never have developed a distorted financial sector. Overconsumption would not have reigned, the currency would not have collapsed, and import problems would not have arisen. It was the Icelandic government's move away from free-market principles and towards government interventionism that set the stage for the spectacular Icelandic tragedy. Only free-market principles and the restoration of property rights in the monetary sphere will prevent such tragedies in the future.

# References

Adrian, Tobias, and Hyun Song Shin. 2008. "Financial Intermediaries, Financial Stability, and Monetary Policy." Paper presented at the Federal Reserve Bank of Kansas City Symposium at Jackson Hole. August 21–23. http://www.kc.frb.org/publicat/sympos/2008/Shin.08.06.08.pdf.

Andersen, Camilla. 2008. "Iceland Gets Help to Recover from Historic Crisis." *IMF Survey Magazine* 37, no. 12. (December 2). http://www.imf.org/external/pubs/ft/survey/so/2008/int111908a.htm.

Aninat, Eduardo. 2001. "IMF Welcomes Flotation of Iceland's Króna." *IMF News Brief* no. 01/29. March 28. http://www.imf.org/external/np/sec/nb/2001/nb0129.htm.

Bagus, Philipp. 2007. "Asset Prices–An Austrian Perspective." *Procesos de Mercado: Revista Europea de Economía Política* 4, no. 2: pp. 57–93.

———. 2009. "Monetary Policy as Bad Medicine: The Volatile Relationship Between Business Cycles and Asset Prices." *Review of Austrian Economics* 21, no. 4: pp. 283–300.

———. 2010. "Austrian Business Cycle Theory: Are 100 Percent Reserves Sufficient to Prevent a Business Cycle?" *Libertarian Papers* 2, no. 2.

Bagus, Philipp, and David Howden. 2009. "Iceland's Banking Crisis: The Meltdown of an Interventionist Financial System." *Ludwig von Mises Institute, Daily Article.* June 9. http://mises.org/story/3499.

———. 2009. "Qualitative Easing in Support of a Tumbling Financial System: A Look at the Eurosystem's Recent Balance Sheet Policies." *Economic Affairs* 29, no. 4: pp. 60–65.

———. 2009. "The Legitimacy of Loan Maturity Mismatching: A Risky, but Not Fraudulent, Undertaking." *The Journal of Business Ethics* 90, no. 3: pp. 399–406.

———. 2009. "The Federal Reserve and Eurosystem's Balance Sheet Policies During the Financial Crisis: A Comparative Analysis." *Romanian Economic and Business Review* 4, no. 3: pp. 165–85.

———. 2010. "The Term Structure of Savings, the Yield Curve, and Maturity Mismatching." *Quarterly Journal of Austrian Economics* 13, no. 3: pp. 64–85.

Bagus, Philipp, and Markus H. Schiml. 2009. "New Modes of Monetary Policy: Qualitative Easing by the Fed." *Economic Affairs* 29, no. 2: pp. 46–49.

Baxendale, Toby, and Anthony Evans. 2008. "Austrian Business Cycle Theory in Light of Rational Expectations: The Role of Heterogeneity, the Monetary Footprint, and Adverse Selection in Monetary Expansion." *Quarterly Journal of Austrian Economics* 11, no. 2: pp. 81–93.

BBC News. 2009. "Iceland Moves Towards Joining EU." July 16. http://news.bbc.co.uk/1/hi/8153139.stm.

Böhm-Bawerk, Eugen von. [1889] 1959. *Capital and Interest.* Vol.2: *Positive Theory of Capital.* South Holland, Ill.: Libertarian Press.

Boorman, Jack. 2000. "On the Financial Role of the IMF." In *Reforming the International Monetary System.* Peter B. Kenen and Alexander K. Swoboda, eds., pp. 366–369. Washington, D.C.: International Monetary Fund.

Borio, Claudio, and Piti Disyatat. 2010. "Unconventional Monetary Policies: An Appraisal." *The Manchester School* 78. (September): pp. 53–89.

Boyes, Roger. 2009. *Meltdown Iceland: Lessons on the World Financial Crisis from a Small Bankrupt Island.* New York, Berlin, London: Bloomsbury USA.

Buiter, Willem H. 2008. "Can Central Banks Go Broke?" *Centre for Economic Policy Research Policy Insight* no. 24 (May).

Buiter, Willem H., and Anne Sibert. 2008. "The Icelandic Banking Crisis and What to Do About It: The Lender of Last Resort Theory of Optimal Currency Areas." *Centre for Economic Policy Research Policy Insight* no. 26 (October).

Calvo, Guillermo A. 1998. "Capital Flows and Capital-Market Crises: The Simple Economics of Sudden Stops." *Journal of Applied Economics* 1: pp. 35–54.

Capell, Kerry. 2008. "The Stunning Collapse of Iceland." *Bloomberg Businessweek* on msnbc.com, October 10. http://www.msnbc.msn.com/id/27104617/.

Capie, Forrest. 1998. "Can There Be an International Lender-of-Last-Resort?" *International Finance* 1, no. 2: pp. 311–325.

Caruana, Jaime, and Ajai Chopra. 2008. "Iceland: Financial System Stability Assessment—Update." IMF Country Report no. 08/368. http://www.imf.org/external/pubs/ft/scr/2008/cr08368.pdf.

Cendrowicz, Leo. 2009. "Iceland's Urgent Bid to Join the E.U." *Time*, July 17. http://www.time.com/time/world/article/0,8599,1911188,00.html.

Central Bank of Iceland. 2001. "New Act on the Central Bank of Iceland." Press Release. November 13. http://www.sedlabanki.is/?PageID=287\&NewsID=25.

———. 2008. "New Rules on Foreign Exchange Balance." Press release no. 18/2008. June 4. http://www.sedlabanki.is/?PageID=287&NewsID=1795.

———. 2008. "Temporary Modifications in Currency Outflow." October 10. http://www.sedlabanki.is/?PageID=287&NewsID=1892.

———. 2009. *Monetary Bulletin* 11, no. 4. http://www.sedlabanki.is/?PageID=1064.

———. 2010. *Monetary Bulletin* 12, no. 2. http://www.sedlabanki.is/?PageID=1095.

Chari, Varadarajan V., and Patrick Kehoe. 1999. "Asking the Right Questions About the IMF." *Federal Reserve Bank of Minneapolis, Annual Report*, pp. 3–26.

Cohen, Daniel, and Richard Portes. 2009. "Toward a Lender of First Resort." International Monetary Fund working paper WP/06/66.

Danielsson, Jon. 2008. "The First Casualty of the Crisis: Iceland." *VoxEU*, November 12. http://www.voxeu.org/index.php?q=node/2549.

Diamond, Douglas W., and Philip H. Dybvig. 1983. "Bank Runs, Deposit Insurance, and Liquidity." *Journal of Political Economy* 91, no. 3: pp. 401–19.

Eichengreen, Barry. 1999. *Toward a New International Financial Architecture: A Practical Post-Asia Agenda*. Washington, D.C.: Institute for International Economics.

Eichengreen, Barry, and Christof Rühl. 2001. "The Bail-In Problem: Systematic Goals, Ad Hoc Means." *Economic Systems* 25, no. 1: pp. 3–32.

Elíasson, Lúdvík, and Thórarinn G. Pétursson. 2006. "The Residential Housing Market in Iceland: Analysing the Effects of the Recent Mortgage Market Restructuring." Central Bank of Iceland Working Paper no. 29.

Engles, Frank. 2001. "Iceland: Selected Issues and Statistical Appendix." IMF Country Report no. 01/82. http://www.imf.org/external/pubs/cat/longres.cfm?sk=4090.0.

Engles, Frank, and Michael Gapen. 2002. "Iceland: Selected Issues." IMF Country Report no. 02/129. http://www.imf.org/external/pubs/cat/longres.cfm?sk=15916.0.

EurActiv. 2009. "Iceland's Parliament Votes in Favour of EU Talks". July 17. http://www.euractiv.com/en/enlargement/iceland-parliament-votes-favour-eu-talks/article-184202#.

Fischer, Stanley. 1999. "On the Need for an International Lender of Last Resort." *Journal of Economic Perspectives* 13: pp. 85–104.

Frankel, Jeffrey A. 1999. "International Lender of Last Resort." Presented at the Federal Reserve Bank of Boston Conference "Rethinking the International Monetary System," June 7–9. http://papers.ssrn.com/sol3/papers.cfm?abstract_id=209318.

Fratianni, Michele, and John Pattison. 2001. "The Bank for International Settlements: An Assessment of Its Role in International Monetary and Financial Policy Coordination." *Open Economies Review* 12, no. 2: pp. 197–222.

Freixas, Xavier, and Jean-Charles Rochet. 2008. *Microeconomics of Banking*. Second edition. Cambridge, Mass.: MIT Press.

Friðriksson, Ingimundur. 2009. "The Banking Crisis in Iceland in 2008." *BIS Review* 22. http://www.bis.org/review/r090226d.pdf.

Fry, Maxwell J. 1992. "Can Central Banks Go Bust?" *The Manchester School of Economics and Social Studies* 60 (Supplement): pp. 85–98.

Garrison, Roger W. 2001. *Time and Money: The Macroeconomics of Capital Structure*. London: Routledge.

———. 2004. "Overconsumption and Forced Saving in the Mises-Hayek Theory of the Business Cycle." *History of Political Economy* 36, no. 2: pp. 323-349.

Gilpin, Robert. 2000. *The Challenge of Global Capitalism: The World Economy in the Twenty-First Century*. Princeton, N.J.: Princeton University Press.

Grauwe, Paul de. 2008. "Returning to Narrow Banking." In *What G20 Leaders Must Do to Stabilize Our Economy and Fix the Financial System*. Barry Eichengreen and Richard Baldwin, eds, pp. 37–39. London: Centre for Economic Policy Research.

Gumbel, Peter. 2008. "Iceland: The Country That Became a Hedge Fund." *CNN Money*, December 4. http://money.cnn.com/2008/12/01/magazines/fortune/iceland_gumbel.fortune/index.htm.

Guðmundsson, Hjörtur J. 2006. "Slashing the Rumors: Iceland is Far From Adopting the Euro." *TEAM Europe*, May 5. http://www.teameurope.info/node/91.

Haarde, Geir H. 2008. "Address to the Nation. Prime Minister's Office." October 6. http://eng.forsaetisraduneyti.is/news-and-articles/nr/3035.

Hayek, F. A. 1931. *Prices and Production*. London: Routledge.

———. [1939] 1975. *Profits, Interest, and Investment*. New York: Kelley.

Honjo, Keiko, and Benjamin Hunt. 2006. "Stabilizing Inflation in Iceland." IMF Working Paper WP/06/262. http://www.imf.org/external/pubs/ft/wp/2006/wp06262.pdf.

Honjo, Keiko, and Srobona Mitra. 2006. "Iceland: Selected Issues." IMF Country Report no. 06/297. http://www.imf.org/external/pubs/ft/scr/2006/cr06297.pdf.

Howden, David. 2010. "Knowledge Shifts and the Business Cycle: When Boom Turns to Bust." *Review of Austrian Economics* 23, no. 2: pp. 165–182.

Hübner, Otto. 1854. *Die Banken*. Leipzig: Verlag von Heinrich Hübner.

Huerta de Soto, Jesús. [2006] 2009. *Money, Bank Credit, and Economic Cycles*. Second edition. Auburn, Ala.: Ludwig von Mises Institute.

Hülsmann, Jörg Guido. 1998. "Toward a General Theory of Error Cycles." *Quarterly Journal of Austrian Economics* 1, no. 4: pp. 1–23.

———. 2008. *The Ethics of Money Production*. Auburn, Ala.: Ludwig von Mises Institute.

Hunt, Benjamin, Robert Tchaidze, and Ann-Margret Westin. 2005. "Iceland: Selected Issues." IMF Country Report no. 05/366. http://www.imf.org/external/pubs/ft/scr/2005/cr05366.pdf.

"Iceland Hunts the Euro." 2009. *The Economist*, January 22.

Iceland Review. 2009. "Salary Cuts for 14 Percent of Wage Earners." January 14. http://www.icelandreview.com/.

International Monetary Fund. 2004. "Iceland—2004 Staff Visit Concluding Statement." October 25. http://www.imf.org/external/np/ms/2004/102504.htm.

———. 2005. "Iceland–2005 Article IV Consultation Concluding Statement." June 13. http://www.imf.org/external/np/ms/2005/061305.htm.

———. 2008. "Iceland: Article IV Consultation–Staff Report; Staff Supplement; Public Information Notice on the Executive Board Discussion; and Statement by the Executive Director for Iceland." IMF Country Report no. 08/367. http://www.imf.org/external/pubs/ft/scr/2008/cr08367.pdf.

———. 2009. "Review of Recent Crisis Programs." September 14. http://www.imf.org/external/np/pp/eng/2009/091409.pdf

Íslandsbanki. 2005. *ÍSB Weekly*, July 26.

Jeanne, Olivier, and Lars E. O. Svensson. 2007. "Credible Commitment to Optimal Escape from a Liquidity Trap: The Role of the Balance Sheet of an Independent Central Bank." *American Economic Review* 97, no. 1: pp. 474–490.

Jónsson, Ásgeir. 2009. *Why Iceland?: How One of the World's Smallest Countries Became the Meltdown's Biggest Casualty*. New York: McGraw Hill.

Kapur, Devesh. 1998. "The IMF: A Cure or a Curse?" *Foreign Policy* 111 (Summer): pp. 114–129.

Knies, Karl. 1876. *Geld und Kredit*. Vol. 2. Berlin: Weidmann'sche Buchhandlung.

"Kreppanomics." 2008. *The Economist*, October 9.

Krueger, Anne O. 2004. "The IMF at Sixty: What Role for the Future?" Lecture at the Central Bank of Iceland, Reykjavik, June 24. http://www.imf.org/external/np/speeches/2004/062404.htm.

Krugman, Paul. 2010. "The Icelandic Post-Crisis Miracle." *The New York Times*, June 30. http://krugman.blogs.nytimes.com/2010/06/30/the-icelandic-post-crisis-miracle/.

Kupiec, Paul. 2003. "Iceland: Financial System Stability Assessment Update, including Report on the Observance and Standards and Codes on the following topics: Banking Supervision, Insurance Regulation, Securities Regulation, Payment Systems, and Monetary and Financial Policy Transparency." IMF Country Report no. 03/271. http://www.imf.org/external/pubs/ft/scr/2003/cr03271.pdf.

Lewis, Michael. [2009] 2010. "Wall Street on the Tundra: The Implosion of Iceland's Economy." Reprinted in *The Great Hangover: 21 Tales of the New Recession*. Graydon Carter, ed., pp. 203-228. New York: Harper Perennial.

Lipton, David. 2000. "Refocusing the Role of the International Monetary Fund." In *Reforming the International Monetary System*. Peter B. Kenen and Alexander K. Swoboda, eds., pp. 345–365. Washington, D.C.: International Monetary Fund.

Mason, Rowena. 2008. "UK Treasury Lends Iceland £2.2 Billion to Compensate Icesave Customers." The Telegraph, November 20. http://www.telegraph.co.uk/finance/financetopics/financialcrisis/3491442/UK-Treasury-lends-Iceland-2.2bn-to-compensate-Icesave-customers.html.

McVeigh, Tracy. 2008. "The Party's Over for Iceland, the Island That Tried to Buy the World." The Guardian, October 5. http://www.guardian.co.uk/world/2008/oct/05/iceland.creditcrunch.

Meese, Richard A. 1990. "Currency Fluctuations in the Post–Bretton Woods Era." *Journal of Economic Perspectives* 4, no. 1: pp. 117–134.

Meese, Richard A., and Kenneth Rogoff. 1983. "Empirical Exchange Rate Models of the Seventies: Do They Fit Out of Sample?" *Journal of International Economics* 14: pp. 3–24.

Milne, Alistair. 2009. *The Fall of the House of Credit. What Went Wrong in Banking and What Can Be Done to Repair the Damage?* Cambridge, UK: Cambridge University Press.

Mises, Ludwig von. [1912] 1953. *The Theory of Money and Credit*. New Haven, Conn.: Yale University Press.

———. [1942] 2007. "Inflation and You." In *Economic Freedom and Intervention: An Anthology of Articles and Essays*. Bettina Bien Greaves, ed., pp. 83-87. Indianapolis: Liberty Fund.

———. 1943. " 'Elastic Expectations' and the Austrian Theory of the Trade Cycle." Economica, n.s., 10, no. 39: pp. 251–252.

———. [1949] 1998. *Human Action: A Treatise on Economics*. Auburn, Ala.: Ludwig von Mises Institute.

Obstfeld, Maurice. 2009. "Lenders of Last Resort in a Globalized World." Keynote address, International Conference of the Institute for Monetary and Economic Studies. Tokyo, Bank of Japan, May 27–28. http://www.imes.boj.or.jp/english/publication/edps/2009/09-E-18.pdf.

Oddsson, Davíð. 2008. "Excerpts: Iceland's Oddsson." *Wall Street Journal*, October 17. http://online.wsj.com/article/SB122418335729241577.html?mod=googlenews_wsj#articleTabs=article.

Ong, Li Lian, and Martin Čihák. 2010. "Of Runes and Sagas: Perspectives on Liquidity Stress Testing Using an Icelandic Example." IMF working paper WP/10/156. http://www.imf.org/external/pubs/ft/wp/2010/wp10156.pdf.

Pétursson, Thórarinn G. 2001. "The Transmission Mechanism of Monetary Policy: Analyzing the Financial Market Pass-Through." Central Bank of Iceland Working Paper no. 14. http://cb.is/uploads/files/wp-14.pdf.

———. 2002. "Wage and Price Formation in a Small Open Economy: Evidence from Iceland." Central Bank of Iceland Working Paper no. 16. http://www.sedlabanki.is/uploads/files/wp-16.pdf.

Preston, Robert. 2008. "Markets Call Time on Iceland." *BBC News*, October 4. http://www.bbc.co.uk/blogs/thereporters/robertpreston/2008/10/creditors_call_time_on_iceland.html .

Rallo, Juan Ramón. 2009. "¿Qué pasó en Islandia?" *La Ilustración Liberal* 41: pp. 43–49.

Rossi, Francesco. 2010. "Iceland's Icesave Referendum: A Possible Outcome Suggested by Electoral Perspective." Working paper. http://www.electoralgeography.com/new/en/wp-content/uploads/2010/03/rossi-iceland.pdf.

Rothbard, Murray N. [1983] 2008. *The Mystery of Banking*. Second edition. Auburn, Ala.: Ludwig von Mises Institute.

Roubini, Nouriel, and Brad Setser. 2004. *Bailouts or Bail-Ins? Responding to Financial Crises in Emerging Economies*. Washington, D.C.: Institute for International Economics.

Shin, Hyun Song. 2009. "Reflections on Northern Rock: The Bank Run That Heralded the Global Financial Crisis." *Journal of Economic Perspectives* 23, no. 1: pp. 101–19.

Stiglitz, Joseph E. 2003. *Globalization and Its Discontents*. New York: W. W. Norton and Company.

Strigl, Richard von. [1934] 2000. *Capital and Production*. Translated by M. Hoppe and H. Hoppe. Auburn, Ala: Ludwig von Mises Institute.

Tchaidze, Robert, Anthony Annett, and Li Lian Ong. 2007. "Iceland: Selected Issues." IMF Country Report no. 07/296. http://www.imf.org/external/pubs/ft/scr/2007/cr07296.pdf.

Thorvaldsson, Armann. 2009. *Frozen Assets: How I Lived Iceland's Boom and Bust*. Chichester, UK: John Wiley and Sons.

Traynor, Ian. 2009. "Iceland to be fast-tracked into the EU." *The Guardian*, January 30. http://www.guardian.co.uk/world/2009/jan/30/iceland-join-eu.

# Index

## A

aid to Iceland
  early requests for liquidity swaps ignored, 97
  from foreign countries, 2–3, 77, 92–94
  from International Monetary Fund, 92, 93, 94
  sought from Russia, 93, 94
Alcoa, 55
Althing
  funds construction of power plants for aluminum smelting, 55
  overspends budget, 4,
  votes for accession talks with European Union, 120
aluminum smelting, 54–55, 94, 106, 117
American Insurance Group, 79
Anti-terrorism, Crime, and Security Act of 2001, 86
Armani, 70
Arnason, Ragnar, 64
Asgeir, Jon, 66

asset prices
  became inflated during boom, 45, 47, 67, 75
  collapsed during crisis, 22–23, 79, 83
Austrian theory of business cycles, 51–54

## B

balance of trade, *see* trade deficit
Bang and Olufsen, 69
Bank of Canada
  inflation-tracking model of, adopted (with adjustments) by Central Bank of Iceland, 16–17
  reduced interest rates during the boom years, 13
Bank of England
  rescues Halifax Bank of Scotland, 79
  reduces interest rates during the boom years, 13–14
  will not establish currency swap with Central Bank of Iceland, 97

Bank of Japan, low interest rates of, 38, 39 fig, 43, 46–47
Banking (Special Provisions) Act, 85
banks, Icelandic, other than Central Bank of Iceland
   and mortgage market, 13, 45, 58–61
   big three banks (Glitnir, Kaupthing, Landsbanki) "too big to fail," 11
   Bunadarbanki, 37
   British newspaper coverage of problems of, 77, 84–85
   maturity-mismatched portfolios of big three, 23 fig
   nationalizing of big three, 2
   net domestic assets and net foreign assets of, 44
   precarious condition of during 2008 liquidity squeeze, 80–84
   privatized in 2003, 4
   ratings of, 37, 42, 75, 98
   recruitment of labor for, 2, 65
   reforms of banking under Prime Minister Davíð Oddsson, 3, 115, 124
   retail banking business of, in Great Britain, the Netherlands, and Germany, 37–38
   shrinking of, following the crisis, 111, 112
   size and growth of, 1, 4
   Sparisjóðabanki, 87
   total assets of big three banks, 96
   total debt of, after the crisis, 89
   see also Glitnir, Kaupthing, Landsbanki
Baugur, 66
Bear Stearns, 76
big three Icelandic banks (Glitnir, Kaupthing, and Landsbanki), see banks, Icelandic, other than Central Bank of Iceland; Glitnir; Kaupthing; Landsbanki
BNP Paribas, 76
Boorman, Jack, on the importance of legal and regulatory architecture to the economy, 31
borrowing in foreign currencies
   by Icelandic banks, 5, 6, 37–38
   for mortgages, 56, 89
   incentivized by stabilized exchange rates, 33, 34, 35
   see also currency mismatching
borrowing short and lending long
   defined, 8 n 5
   see also maturity mismatching
Bradford and Bingley, 79
Brown, Gordon (UK Prime Minister) threatens to sue Iceland and freeze more Icelandic assets, 86
Buffett, Warren, 74
business cycles, Austrian theory of, 51–54

## C

capital, restrictions on moving in and out of Iceland, 91–92
career aspirations and preparation in Iceland turn to banking and finance, 2, 64–65
Caruana, Jaime, 62–63
Central Bank of Iceland (CBI)
   and maturity mismatching, 117
   auctions off its foreign exchange reserves, 103
   interest rates increased by, 75, 77
   interest rates reduced by, 13–14
   liquidity swaps of, 97–98

Central Bank of Iceland (CBI) *(cont.)*
  moral hazard caused by CBI's role as lender of last resort, 10–13, 95–96, 100, 103, 118
  negotiates for Russian loan, 92–93, 98
  not independent of government, 3, 116
  reserve requirements reduced by, 12–13
  restricts purchase of foreign currency, 91
  shortage of foreign reserves, 96–97
  tries to arrest housing boom, 62
  undercapitalized in foreign assets, 100
  *see also* aid to Iceland
Chopra, Ajai, 62–63
Citigroup, 79
credit default swap (CDS), 73–75
credit expansion by central banks
  an instance of maturity mismatching, 8, 24, 117
  and asset prices, 67
  and malinvestments, 51–54, 56
  and stock prices, 71
  artificially lengthens structure of production, 106
  causes business cycles, 116–117
  encouraged by the existence of a central bank that is prepared to help troubled banks, 116
  "exported" via currency mismatching, 42, 43
  fueled international asset-price boom, 67
  impossible under a gold standard, 124–125
  leads to rollover stoppage, 117
  made Icelandic banks vulnerable, 9, 75

credit expansion by CBs *(cont.)*
  magnified by lowering of reserve requirement, 13, 14
  violates depositors' property rights, 116
  *see also* Austrian theory of business cycles
currency mismatching, 5–6, 37–50
  a way to "export" maturity mismatching, 42, 43
  banks thought currency swaps would protect against risks from, 116–117
  consequences when króna declined in value, 77, 81 87, 90
  defined, 38
  encouraged by high foreign exchange rate, 50, 62
  encouraged by stabilized exchange rates and by government or IMF guarantees, 38–39
  IMF recommendations regarding, 42
  made interest rates lower, 56
  profitability of, 38
  would have been prevented under gold standard
currency swaps, 41, 42

# D

Darling, Alistair, UK Chancellor of the Exchequer, 86
De Grauwe, Paul, on maturity mismatching in banking, 10
decadence resulting from inflationary economy, 70
Debenhams, 66
debt, personal, 70, 105
debt-to-equity ratios of Icelandic companies, 71

Diamond, Douglas W. and Philip H. Dybvig on maturity mismatching in banking, 10

## E
EasyJet, 66
egalitarianism of Icelandic society, 56
employment and unemployment, 2, 69, 109, 110, 122, *see also* unemployment insurance; workers, temporary migrant
entrepreneurs need to learn skills to maintain production structure, 106
European Central Bank, 12, 43, 92, 97
European Economic Area, Iceland a member of, 121
European Union, whether Iceland should join or not, 119–124
exchange rate, *see* foreign exchange rate
exports
   aluminum, 54
   lack of capacity to increase, following fall of exchange rate, 112
   seafood, 122
   used cars, 106–107

## F
Fannie Mae (Federal National Mortgage Association), 56
Federal Deposit Insurance Company, 79
Federal Reserve, 13, 14, 43, 78, 92
Financial Services Authority (UK), mentioned, 87
Financial Supervisory Authority (Iceland), mentioned, 84, 85
fishing industry, vi–vii, 107–108, 122
fishing quotas, viii, 107–108
FL Group, 66
Flanagan, Mark, 119

foreign exchange rate, 76 fig
   change to floating rate, 14
   drop in, against Japanese Yen and Swiss Franc, 89
   effect of lower rates on exports, 112
   effect of lower rates on imports, 99
   high and stable rate encouraged currency mismatching, 38–39, 50
   lower since the crisis, 111, 112
   risk from changes in, 33, 117–118
   stabilized, January through Spring 2009, 99–100
   stabilizing, discussed by Iceland and IMF, 92
foreign exchange restrictions, following crisis, 3, 91–92
   exporters use informal offshore markets to avoid, 91
Fortis, 80
Freddie Mac (Federal Home Loan Mortgage Corporation), 56

## G
G20, 31–32
Geyser Crisis, 73–76
glacier bonds, 63
Glitnir
   failure of, 12
   government's plan to support, 83
   put into receivership, 84
   *see also* banks, Icelandic, other than Central Bank of Iceland
gold, price of, 76
gold standard would have prevented Iceland's financial crisis, 124–125
golden rule, 8–9, 10, 74, *see also* maturity mismatching
Goldman Sachs, 79

government ultimately responsible for Icelandic crisis, 3–5, 115–117
Gudmundsson, Bjogolfur, 67

## H
Haarde, Geir
  on his doubts that Iceland should join the European Union, 120
  televised address during financial crisis, 85
Hamleys, 66
Haraldsson, Gunnar, 47
HEKLA, 107
Heritable Bank, 85
Honjo, Keiko, and Benjamin Hunt, 18
Honjo, Keiko, and Srobona Mitra, 18
Housing Financing Fund (HFF), 21, 56–62
housing in Iceland
  boom in, 56, 61–62, 106
  malinvestment in, 54, 55–56
  prices of, 1, 2, 23, 62
  see also Housing Finance Fund; mortgage market
Hübner, Otto, 8
Hülsmann, Jörg Guido, 71
Human Development Index, 1, 40
Hunt, Benjamin, 56
Hypo Real Estate, 80

## I
Icelandair, 66
Icelandic language, marks of the crisis on, 119
Icesave, 76, 85, 93, 94
imports
  increase as resources are shifted to financial industry, 65
  increase because of strong króna, 62, 65
  nature of, 94
  see also trade deficit

inflation
  incentivizes debt, 71
  rate of, 2, 14–20, 44–45, 73, 84, 99
  spurs overconsumption, 69–70
inflation targeting scheme of Central Bank of Iceland, 14–19, 44–45
interest rates
  artificially low worldwide during 2000s, 43, 117
  reduced by several nations' central banks during boom, 13
International Monetary Fund (IMF), 27
  expansion of powers of, 27–28, 29–32
  loss of relevance of, following global shift to flexible exchange rates, 29–30
  moral hazard caused by IMF's role as lender of last resort, 5–6, 28, 32–35, 38–41, 88, 118
  origin and original goals of, 29
  stand-by arrangement between Iceland and International Monetary Fund, 98–99
  talks with Icelandic government about aid to stabilize the króna, 92

## K
Kaupthing
  compensation of directors of, 71
  default of foreign subsidiaries of, 87
  placed in receivership, 87
  profits of, mostly from marking up assets, 71
  see also banks, Icelandic, other than Central Bank of Iceland; Kaupthing Bank Sverige; Kaupthing Edge; Kaupthing Singer and Friedlander

Kaupthing Bank Sverige, 87
Kaupthing Edge, 12, 76, 80, 81, 87, 93
Kaupthing Singer and Friedlander, 40
króna
   shunned by Icelanders after the crisis, 2
   *see also* foreign exchange rate
Krueger, Anne, on IMF's role in preventing and resolving economic crises, 31

## L

labor, *see* banks: recruitment of labor for; career aspirations and preparation in Iceland turn to banking and finance; employment and unemployment; retraining and reassignment of workers; unemployment insurance; workers, temporary migrant
Landsbanki
   assets in Britain frozen, 86
   placed in receivership, 85
   *see also* banks, Icelandic, other than Central Bank of Iceland
Left-Green party against Iceland's joining the European Union, 121–122
Lehman Brothers, 1, 11, 78, 117
Lipton, David, on governments, the IMF, and globalization, 31
liquidity swaps, 92 bis, 93, 94, 97–98, 124,

## M

Magasin du Nord, 66
Magnusson Gylfi, in favor of Iceland's joining the European Union, 121

malinvestments
   in aluminum smelting, 54–55, 94, 106, 117
   in housing, 54, 55–56,
   must be liquidated, 105
   result from credit expansion and maturity mismatching, 6, 9, 25, 47, 52
Mathiesen, Árni, Icelandic Finance Minister, 86
maturity mismatching, 5, 7–8, 101–102, 117–118
   dangers of, 6, 8, 9–10, 22–24
   defined, 7
   distorts structure of production, 24–25
   endorsed by many modern economists, 10
   profitability of, 7–8
   transforms artificial low short term interest rates into artificial low long-term rates, 25
McVeigh, Tracey, on Iceland's financial collapse, 84
Mises, Ludwig von
   on golden rule, 8
   on malinvestments, 52
money market mutual funds, 79
money supply, Icelandic, 12–13, 15, 19–20, 48, 117
moral hazard, *see* under Central Bank of Iceland; International Monetary Fund
Morgan Stanley, 79
mortgage market, 13, 45, 55–63
mortgages denominated in Yen and Swiss Francs become burdensome as króna exchange rate collapses, 89

## N–O–P

Northern Rock, 23–24
nouveau riche Icelanders, 70
Oasis, 67
Oddsson, Davíð
   against Iceland's joining the European Union, 123
   banking sector deregulated and privatized during his time as Prime Minister, 3, 115, 124
   chairman of board of governors of Central Bank of Iceland, 12, 86, 95
   ousted from CBI chairmanship, 116
overconsumption, 68–71
   encouraged by high currency exchange rate, 62
   encouraged by low interest rates, 52–53, 68
   Icelanders must regain their traditional prudence about spending and credit, 105
   would not have occurred under gold standard, 125
Preston, Robert, on Iceland's precarious financial position, 84

## R

recession necessary for Iceland's recovery, 124
recovery of Icelandic economy, 105–125
Rehn, Olli, European Commissioner for Economic and Financial Affairs, on the possibility of Iceland joining the European Union, 122
reserve requirements for banks, 12–13, 14
retraining and reassignment of workers, 108–109, 111
rollover, rolling over of deposits defined, 7, 8
Royal Bank of Scotland, 79
Royal Unibrew, 66

## S

Schengen Area, 120
Shearer, Tony, 71
Sigurðardóttir, Jóhanna, 116, 121
Singer and Friedlander, 71
sovereign bankruptcy, 4, 29
Sparisjóðabanki, 87
"spread" between long-term and short-term interest rates defined, 8
standard of living, in Iceland, 1, 28, 40
State Housing Board, 21
stock market, 2
   boom in, 71–72
   trading suspended for three days, 88
   declines in, after crisis, 88
structure of production, 64, 106

## T

Tatarintsev, Victor I., 92
taxes and contributions to social security in Iceland, 3, 115
Tchaidze, Robert, Anthony Annett, and Li Lian Ong, 56
Thomsen, Poul, on cause of Icelandic financial debacle, 4
Thorvaldsson, Armann
   on his expectation of foreign help for Iceland in case of financial crisis, 40
   on lavish consumption during the boom, 69–70
time structure of production, *see* structure of production
trade deficit, 55, 65, 66 fig, 96–97, 112

## U

unemployment and underemployment, 2, 69, 109, 110, *see also* unemployment insurance

unemployment insurance, 109–111

## W

Washington Mutual, 79
whaling, 121, 122
Wachovia, 79
welfare state, Iceland a, 115, *see also* taxes and contributions to social security; standard of living
Wells Fargo, 79
West Ham United, 67
Westin, Ann-Margret, 56
Woolworths, 66